Discovering the History of Your House

and Your Neighborhood

Discovering
the History
of Your House

and *Your Neighborhood*

Betsy J. Green

SANTA
MONICA
PRESS

SANTA
MONICA
PRESS

Published by:
Santa Monica Press LLC
P.O. Box 1076
Santa Monica, CA 90406-1076
1-800-784-9553
www.santamonicapress.com

Printed in the United States

Santa Monica Press books are available at special quantity discounts when purchased in bulk by corporations, organizations, or groups. Please call our Special Sales department at 1-800-784-9553.

This book is intended to provide general information. The publisher, author, distributor, and copyright owner are not engaged in rendering health, medical, legal, financial, or other professional advice or services. Be aware that offers, phone numbers, addresses, web sites, etc. may have changed. The publisher, author, distributor, and copyright owner are not liable or responsible to any person or group with respect to any loss, illness, or injury caused or alleged to be caused by the information found in this book.

ISBN 1-891661-24-8

Library of Congress Cataloging-in-Publication Data

Green, Betsy J., 1950–
 Discovering the history of your house and your neighborhood / by Betsy J. Green
  p. cm.
  Includes bibliographical references and index
  ISBN 1-891661-24-8
  1. Historic buildings–United States–Research–Handbooks, manuals, etc. 2. Dwellings–United States–Research–Handbooks, manuals, etc. 3. United States Genealogy–Handbooks, manuals, etc. I. Title.

E159 .G686 2002
907'.2–dc21

                2002017600

Book and cover design by Lynda "Cool Dog" Jakovich

Contents

*This book is dedicated
to Von and Alexa*

*and to the memory of Ron E. Nelson,
Historic Preservation Craftsman Extraordinaire
(1937–2000)*

Where Do You Start?

Introduction

☞ *Good for all homes*

Every vintage home has a story to tell. Yours is no exception. Elaborate Victorian mansions, cozy bungalows of the 1920s, and 1950's ranch-style homes – all have a unique history. It's there waiting to be uncovered. This book is your first step on this journey of discovery.

Researching the history of your house is part treasure hunt and part jigsaw puzzle. As you find

If your walls could only talk, what stories they could tell you! Large or small, vintage or not so old, there are all kinds of fascinating facts, legends and lore just waiting to be discovered for every house.

pieces of information, you'll put them together to create a picture of your home's history. You probably won't find the answers to *all* of your questions. But you probably *will* find some fascinating pieces of information that you hadn't even thought about. For example, as you discover information about your house, you will also learn something about the

history of the houses around yours and also the history of your neighborhood.

Wouldn't it be wonderful to move into an older home and find that someone had researched all the previous owners of the home, carefully preserved this information, and recorded any changes that they made to the house? Perhaps they saved photos of snowstorms, weddings, etc. that occurred in the house. Maybe they wrote this information on archival-quality paper and stored it in an acid-free box with suggestions that future owners add their photos, remembrances, and research findings. Every older home should have this kind of information. If your home doesn't, now is the time to start. This book will guide you every step of the way.

Discovering the History of Your House is a starting point – the first step in discovering and preserving the history of your home. If you simply buy this book, keep it in a safe place, and pass it on to the next owner, you have still taken the first step. The research into your home's past is an ongoing process. Do a little here and there when you get the chance, keep careful records of what you've done, and make sure that the next owner inherits your good work.

You are part of your home's history, as is every change that you make to the house. Future owners will appreciate any information that you can pass on to them, whether it is something that you uncovered about your home's past, information about changes you made to the house, or photos of events that took place in your home.

There's a lot of information in this book. Don't let that scare you. Not every section applies to *your* house. The line beneath the section title tells you whether the section applies to your home's age and location. Many sections apply to all homes, but some are more specific. You can decide which sections will help you find the information you want.

You don't have to do everything listed in this book, and you don't have to do it in the order in which it appears. Congratulate yourself for just buying this book and *thinking* about researching the history of your house. It's up to you how much research you decide to do, and how much you leave for future owners of your home.

Some final words of advice as you begin the journey of discovery into your home's past – be patient, be polite, but above all . . . be *persistent.*

Note: I'd love to hear from you! Readers who would like to send me their comments and stories about researching their homes may reach me via e-mail at househistories@hotmail.com.

"... research can be both fun and addictive"
RESEARCHING THE HISTORY OF YOUR HOUSE
COLORADO HISTORICAL SOCIETY

House Research in Your Area

☞ *Good for all homes*

When you start your research, check with your local historical society or museum, library, historical commission, etc. to see if they have a booklet tailored to researching homes in your area. Also talk to organizations at the state level. (See the chapter "Other Sources of Information" on page 201.) This is especially important if you have a really old house – one built before the Civil War era.

———•———

*"All you need is patience, perseverance, and time.
Luck also helps."*
HISTORIC HOUSE RESEARCH HANDBOOK
INDIANA HISTORICAL BUREAU

Getting Started

☞ *Good for all homes*

Don't read this book from cover to cover. Page through it to get an idea of which parts will be useful for you.

The three most important sources of written information about your house are:

1. Deeds
2. Old phone books and city directories
3. Obituaries of former owners

Be suspicious of every fragment of information that you discover about your house. People make mistakes – both in official records and in the things they tell you about your house. If you find a source that says your house was built in a specific year, don't stop your search there. Try to find other pieces of information that corroborate that information.

As you gather information about the history of your home, keep asking yourself, "Does this make sense? Does it agree or conflict with previous information I've found?" If information seems truly contradictory, put it aside for a while and look at it later to see if you gain new insights, or talk to librarians and archivists and ask them for their opinion of what it might mean.

There are three steps to researching the past of your house:

1. Knowing what kinds of information will answer your questions
2. Knowing where to find this information
3. Piecing this information into the unique story of your home's history

Don't be discouraged if you visit a historical society and the volunteers or staff say that they don't have any information about your house. This simply means that they don't have a specific file on your house. (They would only have this information if someone has already researched your home's history. If no one has done this, it's up to you to make a start.)

Create a house history file. Keep track of books that you look at – even the ones that have no useful information. This will save time later if you forget which books you've seen and which ones you haven't.

Even Your Subdivision Has a History

☞ *Good for all urban and suburban homes*

Researching the history of your subdivision or area of town may provide some information about your home or put it in historical context. Sometimes after the plat or map of your subdivision was recorded, local newspapers carried advertisements. Look for these. Also look for brochures, pamphlets, etc. published by the subdivider. You might find these in libraries or historical archives.

"Remember to make your search [for vintage photos] wide enough to include whole neighborhoods in case your particular home might be visible on pictures of a large geographic area (you might even catch a glimpse of the backyard of your house)!"

THIS OLD HOUSE

INDIANAPOLIS-MARION COUNTY PUBLIC LIBRARY

Most homes are in a subdivision. A subdivision is created when someone buys a piece of property and divides it into two or more lots. Many subdivisions cover several blocks, each of which is divided into numerous lots.

How I Got Started

About ten years ago, my family and I moved into an older home. The real estate listing sheet for the home was rather vague about its age. I naively assumed that a quick visit to the local historical society would answer all my questions about the home. (Does this sound familiar?) One of the volunteers at the historical society looked through one file drawer and told me that they had no information about my home.

Determined not to give up, I spent a lot of time figuring out how to research the deeds to our property, and used the information from the deeds as the basis for the rest of my research about my home's past. Eventually I returned to the local historical society armed with a list of all the past owners of my home. This time I found a file on the first owner of my home — Charles Gustafson. I learned that he was a builder who built numerous homes in my town, and built our house for himself in 1908. I also found a late-1800's photo of Mr. Gustafson. When looking through the file of the second family who owned my home, I struck pay dirt. There in the file was a photo of my home dated 1912. The family or a descendant had evidently donated it to the historical society. There was no address on the photo, but I recognized the house as mine.

So it turned out that there was a lot of information about my house in the local historical society's files after all. The volunteer who told me that there was no information on my house had looked for a file with my address on it. There was no file because no one had researched the history of my house — yet.

I enjoyed sleuthing the history of my house so much that I began researching other homes, teaching classes, and writing magazine and newspaper articles on the subject of do-it-yourself house history research. I've researched the history of more than 80 homes that range in age from the 1850s to the 1980s. Each one is different.

Every older home has a story to tell if you know where to look for it, what kinds of information to expect, and know what questions to ask. That's what this book is all about.

Supply List for Beginners

☛ *Good for all homes*

1. A spiral-bound notebook to record your progress and information you've found – keep track of the date you looked for information and where you found information (and where you didn't). A laptop or notebook computer could, of course, take the place of the spiral notebook.

2. A pencil – some libraries and archives that you visit may not allow you to use a pen.

3. A large folder or envelope – legal size is best. Use it to store any loose pieces of paper, your notebook, photos, etc. This will keep all your information in one place.

4. A magnifying glass – this will come in handy when you encounter tiny print or details on a map or other document.

5. Tracing paper – for tracing old maps or surveys that cannot be photocopied because of copyright restrictions.

6. A small stapler – as you accumulate pieces of paper, a stapler will help keep things organized.

"You can figure out a lot if you have a burning desire to know. And I can almost guarantee that you'll have fun doing it."

HOUSE DETECTIVE: GUIDE TO RESEARCHING BIRMINGHAM BUILDINGS

ANN MCCORQUODALE BURKHARDT

> ## Only Believe Half of What You Hear
>
> *While researching an 1895 home, I heard a story that two brothers built the house and lived in it all their lives. Well, after I finished my research, I discovered that the brothers had lived in it all their lives, but they had not built the house — their parents had. So the brothers had been born in the house, and then lived there all their lives.*

"You're Not Using a Pen, Are You?"

☞ *Good for all homes*

Certain research libraries, ones that have lots of valuable materials or books, often have restrictions for researchers. Some are closed-stack libraries. In these, you cannot browse the shelves. You may only be allowed to look through the card catalog or computer catalog and fill out a form for each book. Every 20 or 30 minutes, a library assistant will bring the books to you. You may have to sit and wait at your seat at a particular table in the library.

Most of these libraries forbid you to use pens. Some don't permit book bags or purses. Others don't even allow jackets or bulky cardigans. In some, you can't photocopy materials. You must fill out another form, and a library assistant photocopies materials once or twice a day. Some libraries supply white cotton gloves for you to wear when you handle original materials.

They do all this to protect their valuable and irreplaceable original books and papers.

"Follow That House History Writer"

I often drive around looking at old houses, sometimes snapping pictures and taking notes. I must look suspicious, because I've been stopped a couple of times by police! I suppose they think I'm casing the neighborhood! So, I keep a couple of newspaper clippings about my work in the glove compartment of my car for such occasions. While you might not have any newspaper clippings, it's a good idea to keep some of your research with you to help explain what exactly it is you are doing in case you find yourself in a similar predicament.

Surf the Internet

☞ *Good for all homes*

You'll find several references to helpful addresses on the Internet in this book. More are appearing each month, especially genealogy web sites. Some sites are national in scope; others provide information about a specific state, county, or city. Search for words such as: genealogy, family history, historic houses, historical records, etc. Also try pairing these words with the name of your state or county, such as "morris county AND genealogy." Local colleges and universities may also have useful information that can be located in their online catalogs.

Go to Class

☛ *Good for all homes*

Check at libraries, historical societies or museums in your area to see if anyone offers a do-it-yourself house history class in your area. Such a class can help you get started and give you an idea of the kinds of resources available in your area.

If you can't find a class, ask people if they know of others who have researched houses. Talking with them before you begin your own sleuthing could save you a lot of time.

"Too often researchers are anxious to date their buildings as early as they can. This zeal can lead to inaccurate conclusions if notes are not kept as complete and as clear as possible."
HOW TO RESEARCH THE HISTORY OF YOUR HOUSE (OR OTHER BUILDING) IN NEW ORLEANS
WAYNE M. EVERARD

House Histories Sometimes Mirror Local History

Sometimes the history of the house tells its own story and doesn't need any embellishment. I researched an 1890's house and discovered that the home's history perfectly paralleled the history of the area. The house was built in 1892 as a parish house for the German-language church in the town. That town had originally been settled by German immigrants. By the time the Second World War had ended, the number of German speakers in the area had diminished, the number of church members dwindled, and the parish house was sold. A local couple bought it, and moved it a block away to its current site.

This couple was new to the area, as were many other people who were moving there. They "modernized" the Victorian home the way most people did in the 1940s, by stripping out all the "old-fashioned stuff." When I researched the home, the wife still lived in the home and remembered the elaborate Victorian woodwork with revulsion. "It was the worst dust catcher you ever saw," she complained to me. So, as the area had changed from a German farm community to a bedroom suburb, the house had been changed by its move and its remodeling.

Follow the Paper Trail and the *People* Trail

☞ *Good for all homes*

There are two main sources of information about the past of your home – the paper trail and the *people* trail. The paper trail is all the stuff that has been written down or recorded in photos. The people trail is all the people who have lived in your house or who have known people who lived in your house.

Generally you find the people trail by following the paper trail. The paper trail and the people trail will yield very different kinds of information. The paper trail will tell you who owned your home, who lived in your home, what the sale price was, etc. The people trail will tell you such things as there used to be an apple tree in your backyard that was so beautiful that people came from miles around to see it bloom in the spring, or that a gangster named "Diamond-Tooth Eddy" ran a bootlegging operation out of your house!

If there are older people on your block, in your neighborhood, or at your historical society, ask them about your house. (Bring snapshots of your house with you when you're doing research. People may not know your home's address, but they might recognize it from photos.) If you know the names of the families who used to live in your home, mention these. My house, for example, is known as the

The people who lived in your home in the past can be wonderful sources of information. Even if they lived in your home fairly recently, they may have kept some older photos of the home. Or perhaps they lived in the home when the original owners dropped by one day.

"McDonald's house" because a family by that name lived in it for many years.

When you visit your local historical society, library, or village hall, ask if anyone knows of older people who have lived in your area for a long time. Contacting them might yield some information about your home or the families who lived in it. Sometimes older people in the neighborhood might have old photos that show your house in the background. Ask them about these.

Some day, when you least expect it, someone may knock on your door and tell you that they used to live in your house. (If you know the names of all the people who have owned your home, this would be one way to ensure that the visitors are not prospective burglars!)

If you decide to invite them in, they can often tell you all kinds of fascinating information about your house. Take notes! Ask them if they have any old pictures. Former residents of your house (and their descendants) are the best source of vintage photos of your home.

Reach Out and Touch Someone

While I was researching an 1890's house, I talked to a woman who had lived in the home in the 1940s. She told me that her family had shared a telephone with the family next door. She was not talking about a party line – she meant that they physically shared the phone.

The phone was kept in the neighbor's home. Whenever there was a call for this woman's family,

> *the neighbor would open her window, stick her broom out and tap on this woman's window (the houses were close together) to signal that someone should run over for a phone call!*

Take a Genealogist to Lunch

☞ *Good for all homes*

Much of the research that you will be doing is similar to what genealogists do. If you have a friend or relative who does genealogy research, ask them for ideas about where to look for information. Look up the genealogy group in your area (ask reference librarians if they know of any) and attend some of the meetings to see if anyone can give you any advice. Ask if the group has cataloged or indexed any local newspapers or cemeteries. Some genealogy groups keep their books and files in a certain library. Ask about this as well.

———◆———

"Luck also plays a part in old-house research: A newspaper article about one woman's search for information about her house resulted in a call from an elderly man who had grown up in the house and had photos he was willing to share."

HISTORIC HOUSE RESEARCH HANDBOOK

INDIANA HISTORICAL BUREAU

Don't Believe Everything You Hear About Your House

I researched an 1890's house and the owners had heard that their home had been built by the farmer who also built the home next door. They heard that the farmer built the house next door first, and then built their home for his sister.

Well, it happens that I had also done the history on the house next door, and knew that it had not been built by a farmer. And when I researched the history of this house, it was clear that it had been built earlier than the one next door, that a young couple had built this house, and that there was no farmer or sister involved with either house.

How that story got started, I have no idea. But it just takes one person who misunderstands something or gets something mixed up to get a story like this passed on through the years as though it were gospel.

Historical Information Is Here and There

☞ *Good for all homes*

In this book, I often refer to your local library or historical society, but many times you will find useful information further afield. If the historical society in your city or town does not have what you want (or if there is no historical society in your immediate area), check other historical societies and libraries nearby. Is there a neighborhood association? How about a countywide historical society or museum? What about the historical society or archives for your state? Try contacting the libraries of nearby colleges and universities. Every state has a State Historic Preservation Office (see page 201). The staff in that office can also give you ideas about where to look for information.

More and more organizations are creating online catalogs of their holdings, so ask about information that is available on the Internet. You can also write or call a distant library or historical society if you have a specific question. Directories of museums and historical societies (found at libraries) will give you the addresses and phone numbers of distant historical associations. Or search for addresses and phone numbers on the Internet.

You can also call information and ask if there is a listing for a historical society in the town you want. If the operator cannot find a listing for a historical society or museum in a small town, ask for the phone number of the village hall or public library. Someone there will probably be able to tell you who is in charge of the local historical information.

Don't overlook the power of your local library. Many libraries can locate and order books from all over the United States, or may be able to tell you where to find a copy of a book in your area.

———•———

"Even seemingly meaningless, cryptic notations should be recorded — they may come to have an important meaning as your research continues."

HOW TO RESEARCH THE HISTORY OF YOUR HOUSE
(OR OTHER BUILDING) IN NEW ORLEANS

WAYNE M. EVERARD

Looking At Visual Clues

"What Style Is My House?"

☛ *Good for all homes*

One of the questions that you might have about your house is, "What style is it?" Don't rely on the style that was written in the real estate advertisement or on the listing sheet for your home.

Look for house stylebooks at libraries (call numbers 720–729) or bookstores. The book that is often regarded as the standard is *A Field Guide to American*

Houses by Virginia & Lee McAlester (Alfred A. Knopf, New York, 1991). It's still in print and can be found in or ordered from most bookstores. I like this book because it has many photos of the numerous variations that occur within a particular architectural style. This book also provides information about

Your home's style of architecture can provide another clue to its age. Different styles have been popular during different eras.

the time period when each style was most popular. This can help you pin down the age of your home or the additions made to your home.

Keep in mind that many homes are a combination of two or more styles. This does not mean that something is wrong with your house. Some houses contain elements of an established style and add elements of a new style. Or, a house might have combined the best features of two or more styles. Other houses have had additions or updates over the years.

It's a good idea to be familiar with your home's style so that when you make changes or additions, you'll have an idea of what is and isn't compatible with your home's original style.

Houses Are Not Always What They Seem

Older homes have often been remodeled or added onto several times. One of the more unusual examples I remember is a house in the Art Moderne style. It had sleek, clean lines, smooth walls, lots of windows, and very little trim. An old-timer in the neighborhood told me that the house was actually built in the late 1800s. It had been damaged by fire and had been radically remodeled in the 1940s.

I did a little research at the local historical society and found a newspaper photo of the house just after the fire, and you could see that it was the same house.

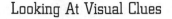

Where Are the Plans for My House?

☞ *Good for all homes*

Many homes never had plans – the builder might have used one set of plans (slightly modified) for numerous houses. If there were plans for your house, the best place to find them would be *in* your house. I've heard of people finding plans in the attic, the basement, or in the back of a closet. Occasionally former homeowners take the plans with them when they move from the house. That's another thing to ask about if you contact former owners of your home or their descendants. Once in a while, people find blueprints at their local historical society or museum.

If you have a house that was built before 1930, you might want to look for books of housing plans that were published when your house was built. Some of these plan books from the late 1800s through the 1920s have been reprinted in recent years, and can be found in libraries and bookstores (see the next section). Note: At some local historical societies, I've seen vintage plan books that were distributed by lumber companies.

Look for Old House Plan Books

☞ *Good for all homes*

House plan books have been around for more than 150 years. Many older homes were built from plan books. These books contained sketches or photos of homes and floor plans. People could send away for the blueprints, and give them to their contractor to build their house. Although many of these books were paperbacks and are not around any more, some have survived, while others have been reprinted.

Libraries and larger bookstores may have copies of reprints of some 1800's and early-1900's house plan books. In libraries, look in the 720-729 numbers; in bookstores, look in the "home decoration," "home repair," or "architecture" sections. It's possible that you might find the plan for your home in these books. Even if you don't find your house, these books often contain sketches or photos showing how the interiors were decorated.

Some newspapers printed house plans – particularly during the booming building years of the 1920s. Look in your local paper in the time period when your house was built. Lumber companies also sold house plans, and would gladly sell customers the lumber that they needed as well. And don't forget historical societies as a source of house plan books.

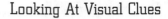

Take Snapshots of Your House

☞ *Good for all homes*

Take some snapshots of the front and sides of your house. They don't need to be award-winning photos – just clear pictures of what your house looks like. These will come in handy when you want to discuss your house with someone – perhaps a librarian or an old-timer in your neighborhood.

Snapshots will also help you remember what your house looks like. Maybe you're wondering if your house is a Sears, Roebuck & Company catalog house, or you're looking at a book and trying to figure out whether your home is a Tudor Revival or a Cape Cod. After you look at numerous pictures of houses, you may begin to forget such details as how many front dormers you have even though you have lived in your home for many years. A few snapshots will help you remember this minutia.

Finding Hidden Treasures In Photo Files

☞ *Good for all homes*

Look for photo files at local libraries, historical societies or museums. If you've researched the deeds to your property, use the list of names of your home's

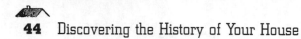

Your house can appear in photos that are indexed under categories other than your address. Search for photos of nearby houses and the families who lived in them — your house could be in the background. Photos of snowstorms or parades could also provide glimpses of your home.

former owners to check the index of photos. In a few areas, there are collections of photos of every building in the town that were taken in the 1930s by Works Progress Administration (WPA) photographers.

If you are really determined to find vintage photos of your home, consider looking at every photo in the collection if the number is not too great. Sometimes photos are not cross-indexed. For example, a photo of people standing on the front steps of your house may be indexed under only one person's name, and that person may not be the homeowner.

Still haven't found a photo? Is your home on a main street? Look at parade photos. Your house might be in the background. Do you live near a park or playing field? Look at sports photos and 4th of July picnic photos. Is your home near a commercial building or a church? Ask them if they have vintage photos that might show your home in the background.

Are there any real estate agencies that have been in your community for a long time? Ask if they have old photos on file. Even 1960's or 1970's photos could be useful if they show your house before the aluminum or vinyl siding went on.

Don't overlook older residents in the neighborhood or their descendants. If someone knocks on your door someday and says that their grandparents used to live in your house, ask them for photos.

———•———

"Often people were photographed within or in front of their homes which then, as now, were a symbol of personal pride and identity."
SOURCES & SEARCHES: DOCUMENTING HISTORIC
BUILDINGS IN NEW MEXICO

FLOYD MCHUGH

Your House Could Be on a Postcard

☛ *Good for all homes built before 1950*
You don't have to live in a big fancy house to find your home on a postcard. When the Eastman

Kodak Company introduced the easy-to-use Brownie Box Camera in 1900, many people began taking photos. This included amateurs (such as homeowners) as well as small-town professional photographers. These were, of course, black and white photos. You could take a photo to the local drugstore, it would be sent off to Kodak, and made into a set of postcards. Houses and people posing on the front steps or porch were popular subjects. (Many of the photos in this book are postcards.)

There were also commercial photographers who took photos of ordinary streets in suburban towns. (They often labeled these with white ink.) These photographers would take the photos and then try to sell them to people in the area.

Be sure to look at any old postcards that your local library or historical society has on file. I've found vintage views of several houses this way.

The fad for turning photos into postcards in the early decades of the 1900s has resulted in a treasure trove of vintage house photos. If you're lucky, you'll find a cryptic hand-written message or a date on the back. Duplicate images glued to a piece of heavy cardboard were used to create a three-dimensional image when used in a stereopticon viewer.

Your chances of finding a postcard increase if your home was formerly a public building such as a parsonage or tea room, or a commercial institution.

It's also possible to find old photos of houses on homemade stereo cards. These are sturdy pieces of cardboard (measuring 4 by 7 inches) that contain two identical photos that were inserted in "stereopticons." Users held this device up close and the photos appeared to be three-dimensional. Most stereo cards were made commercially, but I have found some containing two identical photos of a house pasted on a blank card.

Sometimes you can find postcard dealers at flea markets, antique shops, or postcard shows. Watch for announcements of postcard shows in your local papers wherever antiques or collectible shows are listed. Postcards of houses can be found in categories such as: real photos, photo postcards, architecture, houses, or street scenes. Some postcard dealers organize postcards by state or town, but remember that many homemade postcards are not labeled at all.

———•———

"... fascinating records exist not only for large, imposing homes but for modest ones as well."

HOUSE DETECTIVE: GUIDE TO RESEARCHING
BIRMINGHAM BUILDINGS

ANN MCCORQUODALE BURKHARDT

Finding Your House on Fire Insurance Maps

☛ *Good for all urban and suburban homes built before 1960*

The Sanborn Fire Insurance Company made detailed maps of thousands of towns and cities in the United States beginning in the 1860s. Insurance agents used the maps to assess the fire risk for buildings. This eliminated the need for the agent to visit every property that he or she insured.

The Sanborn Company was the largest, but not the only, fire insurance mapping firm. So if you're not finding any Sanborns at your local library or historical society, ask to see any fire insurance maps. Other fire insurance mapping companies included: Baist, Rascher, and Robinson. These maps were patterned after Sanborn maps, so most of the following information about Sanborns applies to the other companies' maps as well.

The Sanborn Company made new maps on an irregular schedule depending on the growth of the town. The older maps for a given area usually cover only the downtown or commercial area. Later maps cover wider and wider areas. So, if you live near the heart of town, you're most likely to find your house on an earlier map. If you're more than a five-minute walk from the center of town, however, you may not find your house on a Sanborn map until the 1920s or later. Sanborn stopped wide-scale production of maps in the 1950s. If you have an old farmhouse on the outskirts of town, your house may not be on a Sanborn map at all. Sanborn maps are fun because you can watch the development of your neighborhood from one map to the next.

The original Sanborn Fire Insurance Company's maps were contained in large, flat books. They were color coded for brick, stone, or wood exteriors. You can also find Sanborn maps on microfilm, but you can't see the color-coding. Ask at your local library or historical society for fire insurance maps. If they don't have them, try larger libraries at state colleges or universities, or even your state library. If your town formerly had a different name in the past, don't forget to look for Sanborn maps under the former name as well.

The fire insurance maps used abbreviations to indicate the uses of buildings and the materials of which they were made. You might find that your home was once a store, a school, or a boarding house. Look for an explanation of these symbols on the first page of the map because the symbols and their meaning changed slightly through the decades.

Sanborn Maps and Spies

The information on Sanborn Fire Insurance Company maps was so detailed and accurate, that during World War II it was feared that the maps might fall into the hands of enemy agents. I've come across several 1940's Sanborn maps that warn users to keep the maps strictly confidential and not to divulge the contents to "outside interests."

Bird's-Eye Views Are Not Just for the Birds

☛ *Good for urban homes built 1850–1900*

In the second half of the 1800s, thousands of detailed panoramic maps called "bird's-eye views" were created. Artists meticulously sketched every building and tree in a city or town and then created a painting as though the area were viewed from above. These are wonderful sources of information about what houses existed in the year that the view was made. Always ask about these at libraries and historical societies

Never Pass Up an Old Map

☛ *Good for all homes*

Ask to look at all old maps of your area in libraries and historical societies. There are Sanborn Fire Insurance maps, land ownership maps, topographical maps, and other specialty maps. Some early 1900's topographical maps (often produced by the United States Geological Survey) showed the locations of houses and other buildings in rural and suburban areas. Specialty maps include those that show historical sites, patterns of settlement, ethnic settlement areas, etc.

It's a good idea to bring some pieces of tracing paper with you when you go out to do research. Some maps that cannot be photocopied (because they are fragile or copyrighted) can be traced.

Finding the Truth on Old Maps

I found Sanborn maps very useful when I was researching an 1890's house in an urban area. As I was doing the research, I kept coming up with conflicting information about when the house was built on the property. The house that I was researching was built on the back of a corner lot. From looking at the various Sanborn maps, I finally figured out that the house I was researching was the fifth structure built on the property, and that it had formerly been a store.

Don't Overlook
Vintage Aerial Maps

☞ *Good for all homes*

While not as common as bird's-eye view maps, always ask about aerial maps. Some of these were taken from a hot-air balloon, so it is possible to find aerial maps dating back to the 1800s. Aerial maps

A photo taken from a plane or balloon can give you a unique perspective of your house. If you're lucky, you'll find a close-up shot of your home. But even a long-distance photo can help you determine the existence of your home at a certain date.

can be useful in discovering the existence and/or appearance of your home at a specific date.

How Was My House Decorated When It Was Built?

☞ *Good for all homes*

Once you figure out the general time period that your house was built, you might be curious about how it was decorated. Look for books about interior designs of the Victorian era, and the Arts & Crafts period of the early 1900s in your local library

Interior photos are rare, but magazines and newspapers that were published when your house was built can provide a wealth of information about vintage interior decorating schemes.

in the 720–729 numbers in non-fiction. Similar books can be found in the collections of historical societies, and at larger bookstores.

For authenticity, you can't beat what researchers call primary sources – materials written at the time. These include magazines, catalogs, and newspapers. There have been magazines dealing with interior décor since before the Civil War. You'll find ideas both in the editorial and advertising pages of magazines and newspapers. Some newspapers had a "ladies page" that contained decorating ideas or sketches of interior designs. Look for the following magazines on microfilm at larger libraries:

American Architect
American Architect and Architecture
American Architect and Building News
American Builder
American Homes and Gardens
Architectural Forum
Architectural Record
Architecture and Building
Better Homes and Gardens
Cosmopolitan
Country Life in America
Godey's Magazine
House and Garden
House Beautiful
Ladies Home Journal
Redbook

The above list is by no means complete. Look for vintage decorating magazines that were published locally as well.

You might also visit historic house museums that are similar in age to your own house. These can also provide ideas about how your house was first decorated. Information about historic house museums may be found in travel guides, historical societies, visitors' bureaus, and directories of museums (ask at your local library). Also try the Internet.

Sometimes a local historical society's vintage photo collection includes interior shots of older

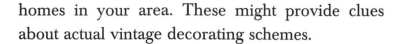

homes in your area. These might provide clues about actual vintage decorating schemes.

Using Vintage Architectural Magazines

☞ *Good for all homes*

Many homes were built from plans that were printed in mainstream magazines and architectural and trade journals. While you may not find the exact plans for your house, you will probably find something similar, and learn how homes were built at that time.

Look for vintage magazines on microfilm at large libraries in cities and universities. There were hundreds – some were national, some were regional. Some also changed names over the years.

Use the following lists of words to search for magazine titles in library catalogs. Once you've found a magazine title, check to see if it was published when your house was built. You can eliminate some of the words if they don't apply to your house. For example, if you have a frame house with a concrete block foundation, you can skip "Brickbuilder." If you're not interested in vintage plumbing fixtures, skip "Sanitary."

Look for vintage magazines containing with these words:

Architect/s
Architectural
Architecture
Artisan
Brickbuilder
Bricklayer
Brickmaker
Builder/s
Building
Carpenter/s
Carpentry
City
Clay
Commerce
Construction
Contractor
Decorator/s
Design/s
Domestic
Engineer
Engineering
Farmer
Financial
Garden/s
Gardening
Home/s
House/s
Iron
Ladies

Landscape
Lumber/man
Manufacture/r
Manufacturing
Modern
Real Estate
Review
Sanitary
Stone
Technology
Wood/worker
Workshop

In addition, try putting any the following words in front of the above words (for example – "Southern" + "Brickbuilder"):

American
Bulletin of
Dixie
East Coast
Inland
Journal of
National
Northwestern
Pacific
Prairie
Southern
West Coast
Western

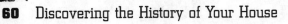

(your city name)
(your state name)

Searching for Physical Clues

If Your Walls Could Talk

☛ *Good for all homes*

Archeological finds are not just limited to the outdoors. Look carefully for clues to the past of your home when you make repairs or do renovation work. Plasterers often signed and dated their work. Window installers sometimes put a newspaper in the wall. Occasionally, people living in a home would write their names on walls and add some information about national or local news as well. Photograph any of your finds before you paint or remove them. I've seen some homes where people can't bear to cover up an old inscription on the wall, so they build a frame around it with a glass cover, and then paint or paper around the frame. Be sure to alert contractors working on your home that you are interested in historical items.

Consider signing and dating any work that *you* do on the house. You might want to include an informal time capsule inside a wall as well. You can include such items as letters from you or your children to future owners, copies of current newspapers, small toys, photos, etc. Store these inside a heavy-duty plastic storage bag that zips shut.

Does Your Home Have a Secret Room?

I always try to tour the inside of the homes that I research. This is one of the best parts of my job. One of the more interesting homes I've been inside was an 1852 house that had been owned by a banker.

This house contained a closet that had been converted into a vault complete with a steel door, cement floor and ceiling. But even more remarkable – the home had a secret room that the homeowners didn't discover until six months after they had moved in! The room was actually part of the attic, but it was not accessible from the attic and you didn't really notice it when you were in the attic – it was an old house with lots of interesting nooks and crannies.

The owners discovered the room when some young relatives were visiting and asked if they could explore. In one bedroom, there was a built-in wardrobe with cabinets above that could only be reached by ladder. The kids got a ladder and opened all the cabinet doors. Behind one they found an eight-foot square room. No one knows for sure why the secret room is there, but it might have been used for storing furs, jewelry, silver, and other valuables. That's what I love about old houses – they're all different and they all have their secrets.

Do You Have a Sears Catalog House?

☛ *Good for all homes built 1908–1940*

From 1908 to 1940, Sears, Roebuck & Company sold approximately 100,000 homes by catalog. There were about 450 different styles – from large to small. Houses ranged from modest cottages, to farmhouses, to elaborate Colonial Revival homes. All the pieces of the home were shipped by rail, so you can find Sears houses wherever you can find a railroad.

All of the lumber was cut to size at the factory. This was a great savings in time and money because many suburban towns did not have electricity 24 hours a day until the 1920s, and electric-powered tools could not be used. If you or your contractor had to saw every board by hand, it was very time consuming.

Every piece of lumber in a Sears house had a number stamped on it, and assembly was required. (If you think assembling a tricycle on Christmas Eve is a challenge, imagine putting together a whole house with thousands of pieces!)

Many people learn that they have a catalog house when they or a contractor tear things apart and find numbered pieces. Some Sears houses have plumbing fixtures or other pieces of hardware with the Sears name on it or simply "SR." Occasionally people find a shipping label from Sears attached to a board in the attic or basement.

The book *Houses By Mail* (Katherine Cole Stevenson & H. Ward Jandl, Preservation Press, Washington D.C., 1986), contains all the various models of Sears homes. There is also a reprint of the 1926 edition of the Sears home catalog *(Sears, Roebuck Catalog of Houses 1926*, Dover Publications, NY, 1991). Another book called

Houses in a Box (Schiffer Publishing Ltd., Atglen, PA, 1998) contains model homes from Sears catalogs of the early 1900s.

The Mystery of the Name on the Window

I once researched an 1890's home that had a curious story relating to a windowpane. At one point in the past, so the story went, the maid who worked in the home had scratched her name in the kitchen window. The owners preserved this piece of glass even when they redid the kitchen. But it always struck me as an odd thing for a maid to do. I could picture the lady of the house, perhaps as a new bride, feeling excessively possessive about her new home and writing her name on the window. But why would a maid do it?

I discovered the answer when I managed to track down a woman who had married one of the boys who had grown up in the house. Her husband told her that when he and his brothers were in their teens, the maid became engaged. They teased her saying that her diamond engagement ring wasn't the real thing. To prove to the boys that it was, the maid took off her ring, and wrote her name in the kitchen window.

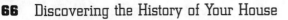

Did Your Home Come from Another Catalog Company?

☞ *Good for all homes built 1900–1950*

If you think you have a Sears, Roebuck & Company house (or an older neighbor has told you that you have one), but you can't find it in any of the Sears books (see the previous section), it may be from another catalog company. Montgomery Ward in Chicago made Wardway Homes. Aladdin and Lewis Manufacturing (Liberty Homes) – both located in Bay City, Michigan – made catalog homes, and so did Gordon Van-Tine in Davenport, Iowa. There were other smaller companies as well.

These companies' pre-cut catalog homes are not as well-documented as Sears homes. One of the best sources of information about these lesser-known catalog homes is a book titled *America's Favorite Homes* (Robert Schweitzer & Michael W.R. Davis, Wayne State University Press, Detroit, 1990).

Other books to look for include:

117 House Designs of the Twenties (Gordon-Van Tine Co., Dover Publications, NY, 1992)

Gordon-Van Tine Co.: Architectural Details 1915 (American Life Foundation, Watkins Glen, NY, 1985)

Aladdin "Built in a Day" House Catalog, 1917 (Dover Publications, NY, 1995)

Aladdin Homes 1918–19 (American Life Foundation, Watkins Glen, NY, 1985)

Bennett's Small House Catalog, 1920 (Dover Publications, NY, 1993)

The Porch Swing That Was Meant to Be

There are two kinds of old homeowners: Those who have vintage photos of their home, and those who want vintage photos of their home. I once researched an old house whose owners were hoping to find vintage photos that would show what the home looked like before it was covered with aluminum siding. The owners planned to remove the siding, and return the home to its original appearance.

I finally managed to find the grandson of the home's first owners. He lived in California, so I wrote to him and explained who I was and why I was looking for old photos of the house. I also sent him some information that I had found about his grandparents. I wrote to him three times before I received a response.

He kindly sent me a photo and two postcards of the house. The photo showed his mother and grandmother sitting on a swing on the front porch. It's a lovely photo of a woman and a girl in long white dresses and black stockings sitting on the swing. What's amazing about this photo is that the original swing disappeared decades ago, but the home's current owners had recently installed a porch swing in the same spot without knowing about the original swing!

Have You Tried a Metal Detector in Your Yard?

☞ *Good for all homes*

Renting or borrowing a metal detector and searching your yard for items left behind by previous occupants of your home can yield interesting "treasures." Children might have lost lead soldiers in the grass, and housewives often burned or buried trash in the decades before regular garbage pickups began.

You might also unearth items when digging in your garden. Finding lumps of coal near a basement wall could indicate the location of an old coal scuttle.

Be careful not to leap to conclusions over your "finds," however. Discovering an 1860's coin does not mean that your house dates to that era. Remember that before your house was built, the land was probably a vacant lot where neighborhood children played, or local people walked through while taking a short cut.

Label your "finds," and store them in archival containers for future owners. Or you may wish to take photos of excavated items and donate the items to the local historical society.

"Each property in the built environment has stories to tell."

HOW TO RESEARCH THE HISTORY OF REAL ESTATE

CHARLOTTE-MECKLENBURG HISTORIC LANDMARKS COMMISSION

Finding antique toys on your property, with the aid of a metal detector, can provide a tangible link to the former occupants of your home.

Front Doors in the Basement

The older the basement, the more likely it is to have something interesting in it. In the basement of an 1860's home that I was researching, the owners showed me the original front doors down in the basement. They had been removed years ago and had been made into partitions in the basement. Apparently there had been an apartment in the basement during the 1930s or 1940s. The owners have since restored the doors. That's something to think about if you find an item in your house that does not belong in its present location. Perhaps it came from elsewhere in the house.

Digging Up the Past in Old Privy Holes

☞ *Good for all homes built before 1900*

If your home was built before indoor plumbing was common in your area, there was probably an outhouse in the backyard. This was generally a small wooden structure placed over a pit. In addition to being used as a toilet, privies often served as the repository of fallen items such as shoes or jewelry, or discarded items such as broken dishes or whiskey bottles.

A new privy hole had to be dug every ten years or so, generally near the older hole. You may have

more than one of these potentially interesting archeological sites on your property. They were generally situated on the opposite side of the yard from the well, not too far from the house, and generally downwind from the house – for obvious reasons. Some families also planted a lilac or other bush with fragrant flowers near the outhouse.

Contact local historical societies, as well as bottle collector organizations, to find someone in your area who is knowledgeable about finding and excavating old privy holes.

Again, keep your "archeological finds" in archival containers, and write down when and where you found the items. Donate the items to your local historical society or museum, or leave them for your home's future owners.

A House-Raising Story

While researching a 1906 house, I managed to track down the grandson of the family that had built the home. He told me that about 1910, his grandparents had jacked up the house and added a new first floor, turning the one-and-a-half-story home into a two-and-a-half-story home.

That's the kind of interesting information that you don't find in the public records, and it's not something that would occur to us today. Of course, the current owners had no idea that the first floor of their home was not as old as the second floor.

Was Your House Ever Moved?

☞ Good for all homes

How can you find out if your house was ever moved from another location? First of all, you might ask your neighbors. If your basement appears to be newer than the rest of your home, it could be that it was an older home that was moved to its present site. Sanborn Fire Insurance maps of the area might also provide clues. (See the section *Finding Your House on Fire Insurance Maps* on page 48.) If your home is clearly Victorian, but no house appears on your lot on older maps, perhaps your house was moved.

Where was your house moved from? Often it came from a nearby location. If your home has a distinctive outline or footprint, look at Sanborn maps to see if there was a house with that same profile somewhere else on the same block. If *that* house is no longer in its original location, perhaps it was originally *your* house.

If your home was moved from another location (usually in your town), the increase in value from one deed to the next could indicate when the house arrived on your property. That may be your only clue.

If you want to know about the history of your house before it was moved to your property, you will have to know exactly when it was moved and its precise former location. If you know this, you can look at the deeds for *that* piece of property for the time that your house was located there and, perhaps, learn more about the people who owned your home in its former existence.

Once your home was moved to its present site, the deeds for *your* property will pertain to the homeowners after the move. If you don't know where your house came from, it's doubtful that you will ever know more about it. But, you never know, sometimes information turns up in items donated to the local historical society, and someday someone who lived in the area years ago may knock on your door. Ask around at the historical society to see if there are any people still in your area who might recall the house being moved. The *people* trail is often the best source of information about relocated houses.

House Moving Stories

House movings did not always go smoothly. In researching a house that had been moved, I contacted an old timer in the neighborhood. Not only was he able to tell me about the house I was researching, but he also shared the story of another house that he himself had moved. He said that in the 1950s, he had moved an 1860's house to his property, but when the mover was putting the house on the new foundation, half of the house collapsed. So he rebuilt that half of the house. The result is a house, half of which dates to the 1860s and half dates to the 1950s. Imagine the plight of some future owners trying to figure out the age of that home!

Houses were moved quite often in the 1800s and early 1900s. In fact, in the mid-20th century, many homes were moved out of the path of super-highways. But it was easier to move homes in the 1800s when there were fewer plumbing, heating, or electrical connections. There were also far fewer (or no) electrical lines to be raised en route. One of the biggest expenses when a house is moved today is paying to raise and lower utility lines.

I know of an old house with a chimney in the upstairs closet. The chimney is not attached to any fireplace or furnace and does not extend down to the first floor. The owners couldn't figure out why until they heard that the house had been moved from another location. The chimney must have been cut off after the move.

Some houses were moved in a very simple fashion. Holes were knocked in the foundation (assuming there was a foundation), and logs were placed under the house to act as rollers. Then oxen or horses (and later tractors or trucks) would pull the house to its new location. The slang term for this was "shed dragging."

The more sophisticated method used flat-bed wagons or trucks to move the house, and sometimes houses were floated on barges down rivers or canals. Some people used a mechanical device with pulleys that enabled just one horse to do the pulling. City directories often contained ads for house-moving companies.

It might take several days for a house to move a mile or so. Since the movement was so slow, people often continued to live in the homes as they were pulled along. Some threw house-moving parties that lasted for days.

House moving occurred frequently in cities where property values were rising rapidly. A person might buy a lot near the heart of town when the city was young and put a house on it. Then the value of the lot might increase so much that, in a few years, it would be profitable to sell the lot and move the house further away from the city center where land was cheaper.

Uncovering the Original Colors of Your Home

☞ *Good for all homes*

Although it's possible to find vintage color photos of your home, it's not very likely. Even if you did, color photos fade over time.

Black and white photos can provide some information about how your house was painted years ago, but scraping or sanding through layers of more recent paint will reveal the original color scheme.

Assuming that the original paint was not stripped off your home, you can use a sander, sand paper, paint scraper or razor-blade cutting tool in an inconspicuous spot to scratch through the layers of paint. The first coat of paint put on the house was probably primer, so look at the paint color immediately on top of that. Most paints fade and yellow over time, so try to do this in a place that is relatively protected from the elements. Inside your home, you might find vintage paint colors or wallpaper behind or under trim, switch plate covers, radiators, etc.

You Never Know What You'll Find in an Old Basement

When I visit an old house, I always ask to look at the basement because I can see the construction methods and materials more clearly down there. One of the strangest things that I've ever seen was a tree stump in an 1870's basement. The original part of the house was built over a basement, but the addition was built over a crawl space. There must have been a tree close to the house that was cut down to make way for the addition, and the people building the addition didn't feel it was necessary to take out the tree stump, so it's still there.

And who knows what else is there? This house was formerly a parsonage. The owners have heard that the yard was originally used as a graveyard. Later, when a cemetery was established, the graves were moved, but there was a story that one of the graves, that of an old French fur trader, could not be moved. So maybe he's down by the tree stump. Who knows?

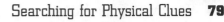

My Home's Not Historic, But I Want to Fix It Up Right

☞ *Good for all homes*

Just because your house is not included on any historic lists or registers, doesn't mean that you cannot treat it as if it were a historic home. Some general guidelines of do's and don'ts are contained in a document called *The Secretary of the Interior's Standards for the Treatment of Historic Properties with Guidelines for Preserving, Rehabilitating, Restoring & Reconstructing Historic Buildings.*

As you may have guessed by the name, this is a government publication. It discusses, in very general and often repetitive terms, how to care for historic

Finding a vintage photo of your home may inspire you to recreate long-lost details that were removed in a 1960's "remuddling."

buildings. The *Standards* are intended to be used by owners of buildings listed on the National Register of Historic Places, but can provide guidance for all vintage homeowners. You can access this report on the Internet at www2.cr.nps.gov/tps/secstan1.htm. If you can't find this through your local library, contact your State Historic Preservation Office.

More specific information about using appropriate methods for preserving your vintage home can be found in a series of publications from the National Park Service – the *Technical Preservation Briefs*. This is a series of booklets on specific topics that might interest vintage homeowners:

1. *The Cleaning and Waterproof Coating of Masonry Buildings*
2. *Repointing Mortar Joints in Historic Brick Buildings*
3. *Conserving Energy in Historic Buildings*
4. *Roofing for Historic Buildings*
5. *Preservation of Historic Adobe Buildings*
6. *Dangers of Abrasive Cleaning to Historic Buildings*
7. *The Preservation of Historic Glazed Architectural Terra-Cotta*
8. *Aluminum and Vinyl Siding on Historic Buildings*
9. *The Repair of Historic Wooden Windows*
10. *Exterior Paint Problems on Historic Woodwork*
11. *Rehabilitating Historic Storefronts*
12. *The Preservation of Historic Pigmented Glass* (vitrolite and Carrara glass)

31. *Mothballing Historic Buildings*
32. *Making Historic Properties Accessible*
33. *The Preservation and Repair of Historic Stained and Leaded Glass*
34. *Applied Decoration for Historic Interiors Preserving Composition Ornament*
35. *Understanding Old Buildings: The Process of Architectural Investigation*
36. *Protecting Cultural Landscapes: Planning, Treatment and Management of Historic Landscapes*
37. *Appropriate Methods for Reducing Lead-Paint Hazards in Historic Housing*
38. *Removing Graffiti from Historic Masonry*
39. *Holding the Line: Controlling Unwanted Moisture in Historic Buildings*
40. *Preserving Historic Ceramic Tile Floors*
41. *The Seismic Retrofit of Historic Buildings: Keeping Preservation in the Forefront*
42. *The Maintenance, Repair and Replacement of Historic Cast Stone*

All of the above publications are available online at: www2.cr.nps.gov/tps/briefs/preshom.htm or can be ordered by mail through this web site. (The online versions of these briefs do not have the photos and illustrations that you would get if you ordered the printed versions.)

Using Your Address to Find Info

Who Was the Architect for My Home?

☞ *Good for all homes*

Most homes were not custom designed by an architect (the technical term for such homes is "vernacular").

Your house may have been built by plans bought from a plan book company, provided by a catalog company, or the builder may have used or modified one plan for several houses. Most of these plans were originally created by architects who sold the rights to their designs.

The original building permit for your home, if it still exists, might have the name of the architect on it. (See the section "Locating Building Permits for Your House" on page 85). If you have a large, historic home, there might have been a notice in a building or architectural magazine about your home when it was first built. If you're lucky, the architect's sketch or a photo of your newly completed home was published in an architectural magazine. Refer to the section "Using Vintage Architectural Magazines" on page 57 for a list of magazine titles to look for.

If you know when your house was built, you might find mention of the architect's or builder's name in a local newspaper that was published at the time. Also note that many local papers had a gossip column that sometimes mentioned the construction of homes, in addition to all kinds of fascinating minutiae about the doings of the local citizens.

Locating Building Permits for Your House

☞ *Good for urban and suburban homes built after 1890*

Visit the building department in your city or town (for rural areas, try the county), and ask to look at any building permits on file for your address. (Building departments are sometimes called "code enforcement" or "planning departments.") Make copies of any permits that you find for your address.

Examine the permits carefully for names of homeowners and any architects involved. If you're lucky, you might find the original building permit for your home with its price. If you're very lucky, you might find a copy of an old survey of your home that shows its footprint before any additions were made.

It's possible that there may not be any building permits for your home. Sadly, some municipalities discard these records after several years. But you never know what's there until you look.

Don't be concerned if you are told that you cannot see any building permits unless you fill out a *Freedom of Information Form.* The FOI forms are usually very simple, and generally ask for information such as your name, address, phone number, and what kind of information you want to see. Sometimes the clerk will ask you to come back in a week.

Don't Let FOI Forms Scare You

When I go to a village or town's building permit department and ask to look at the permits on file for a house that I am researching, I am often asked to fill out a Freedom of Information (FOI) form. For some reason, the clerks often put on their best John Wayne imitation and say, "Well, you'll have to fill out a Freedom of Information form" as if that will make me turn around and run out of the office. Maybe that's what they're hoping I will do.

One clerk, when I asked to look at some building permits, looked me right in the eye and said with finality, "You can't see them because you don't have a Freedom of Information form." If I hadn't asked her where I could get one, she clearly wouldn't have told me.

A Freedom of Information form sounds scary, but it's usually a fill-in-the-blank form asking for your name, address, and what information you want to look at. No big deal.

Utility Records Can Provide Clues

☛ *Good for urban and suburban homes built after 1880*

In some towns, you can access records that show when your home was first connected to the public water, sewer, or electrical systems. These records are usually fairly accurate. But remember that your home could have been built *before* these systems existed. In such cases, the date of connection will *not* indicate the construction date.

Finding the Original Price of Your Home

☛ *Good for urban and suburban homes*

One official source that is usually pretty accurate is the building department in your city or town. Sometimes this department is called "code enforcement." There may be a file on each house on microfiche. Any copies of permits on the house, whether for a fence or addition or whatever, would be in this file. If you find the original building permit for your house, it could contain the original cost of the house.

Local utility companies sometimes keep records of the installation dates of water or electrical connections on a street-by-street or house-by-house basis.

If you live out in the country or in an unincorporated area, you may not find a building permit. Some cities began requiring building permits in the 1800s, but many suburban towns did not start until zoning began in the 1920s. Not all municipalities save vintage building permits, but it's worth asking about them.

Contact Local Insurance Companies

☞ *Good for all homes built after 1900*

There can be useful information in the historical records of local insurance companies. Contact companies that have been active in your area for a long time. Their records might include floor plans, and dates of insurance coverage might help pinpoint when a house was first built.

Thank the Taxman!

☞ *Good for all homes*

In some areas, you can find year-by-year information about the taxes that were paid on your property. These records often included the assessed value and the name of the person who paid the taxes. The records might be in the form of old books, appraiser cards, or might be on microfilm. The assessment might have been done at the city, township, or county level.

Every piece of property should have its own unique identifying number. This number may be called a tax unit number, property identification number, or parcel ID number. This may help you locate the tax records for your house. Tax records may also be indexed by your property's legal description.

Look for tax records in your County Revenue Department, Tax Appraiser's Office, County Tax Office, Office of the Ordinary, or Judge of Probate. Some historical tax records may be kept in the City Clerk's Office, City Hall, or your state's historical archive.

Tax records are most useful when viewed in sequence over a period of years. A jump in the value of your property (when nearby properties do not show a similar increase) could pinpoint the year that the house was built. Remember that the taxes for any given year reflect the value of the property in the *preceding* year.

If the tax records for your property give the construction date of your house, don't trust it until you've compared it with other information that you've found for your house.

―――――•―――――

"Trust the accuracy of any source until you can prove otherwise, but do not ever close yourself off to contradictory evidence."
UNCOVERING THE HISTORY OF YOUR HOUSE
RHODE ISLAND HISTORICAL SOCIETY

Tax Records Can Be Misleading

You should try to confirm any piece of information that you've found about your home's past with other information. Official sources are no more reliable than any other sources.

Once, I was trying to figure out the year that a late 1800's house had been built. The property changed hands in 1893 for $800 (this would buy a nice-sized lot in that town), and in 1895, the appraised value of the property increased six times. Based on this information, I was pretty sure that the house had been built in 1894. Because the property was near the center of town, the area was included on the 1892 Sanborn Fire Insurance Company map. And, lo and behold, there was the house in 1892, contradicting my conclusion based on the deed price and the year the value increased. What happened?

> *I'll probably never know for sure, but I have heard that people sometimes put a false (low) price on a deed so that the tax assessor would not know that a house had been built on the property and would not raise the tax. Apparently, in 1894, the assessor somehow discovered that a house had been built on the property and increased the assessed value.*

Ask for Street and House Files

☞ *Good for urban and suburban homes*

You might be lucky to live in an area where there is a file for every street or house at the local library or historical society. Look at all the information in the files that contain information about your house or street and make photocopies of any relevant information. These files can contain very useful data.

Sometimes there are clippings from local papers about work done on the home, or about the activities of people who lived in your house. This is often one of the only places that you can find information about families that rented your house.

If you live in an area where the deeds are filed by grantor (seller) and grantee (buyer) names, finding information about past owners of your home can help if one or more deeds have not been

Your home may have had another address years ago, especially homes located on a corner. The old address may have had a different house number and may have used the other street as its address.

recorded. Knowing an owner's name can provide a name to search for in the index books.

Note: If your house is on a corner lot, keep in mind that it might have had an earlier address on the other street.

Just Because It's Written Down, Doesn't Mean It's True!

You should not trust everything that you read in official sources. Most people who say they know when their house was built got the year from the real estate listing sheet when they bought their house. This date usually comes from the tax assessor's records, and in my experience, these dates are wrong about half the time — by as many as 20 years, in either direction.

I once called a township assessor's office and asked for the date of a house. The person who answered told me it was built in 1915. This was so far off that I talked to them about it, and said there was no way this house could have been built that late. The person talking to me said, "Well, we didn't keep those records until the 1950s, and at that point, someone rode around and guessed at the date of all the pre-existing houses."

So you can imagine two guys driving around in a township truck, saying, "Well Vern, what date shall we give this house?" and Vern says "How about 1915, Al?" And Al says, "Sounds good to me." So they write it on the form, and suddenly it's official!

If the assessor's date for your home makes sense to you, it may be correct. But if several other pieces of evidence point to another date, remember that the assessor's date could be wrong.

Is Your Home in a Subdivision?

☞ *Good for all homes*

You'll find the answer to this question on your current deed. Look at the description for your property. If you are in a subdivision, your legal description will include the name of the subdivision, the block number and the lot number (or numbers) of your property. For example, it might read: "Richardson's Subdivision, block 12, lot 82"; or "Lots 3 and 4 in Sweet Homes Subdivision." In some cities, your property description might also include your square number.

When someone subdivides a piece of land into streets, blocks, and lots, he or she generally records a map ("plat") of the subdivision. Often this is filed in the same office where deeds are filed. Looking at the original plat map of your subdivision might provide some clues about the history of your house. If your house seems to be about the same age as most of the other homes on your block, they were all probably built *after* the land was subdivided. There are exceptions, of course. If your house looks like an old farmhouse, and all the houses around you are much newer, your home could have been the original farmhouse in the area, and the other homes may have been built later by the subdivider.

Land that has not been subdivided has a longer and more complicated legal description that might read something like "the east half of the northeast quarter of Section 12, township 3, range 11 in Northfield Township" or it may be even more complicated and contain a long paragraph with references to readings on a compass. Read the sections "N 18.5 Degrees 3 Chains 5 Links" and "North 15 Degrees East 13 Chains, East 8 Chains . . ." on pages 184–185 for more information about sorting out these descriptions.

Remember: Tell every reference librarian, historical society volunteer, etc. what kinds of information you are looking for, and ask if they have any advice about where to look or who to ask.

Is Your Home Listed on an Architectural Survey?

☞ *Good for all homes*

Ask at local libraries, historical societies or museums, as well as city and state historic commissions and preservation associations about architectural surveys of your area. Nationwide there is the Historic American Buildings Survey that first began in 1933. Look for this at larger archives or libraries, ask your local library to order it for you, or contact your State Historic Preservation Office (see page 201).

Also try the Internet at www.cr.nps.gov/habshaer/ coll/index.htm.

Some states have conducted their own surveys. In Connecticut, for example, more than half of the towns in the state are included in Town Architecture Surveys, and more than 90,000 properties were surveyed for the Statewide Historic Resource Inventory. In some other states, the Works Progress Administration (WPA) surveyed and described existing houses and buildings in the 1930s. Check also to see if any preservation or landmarks groups in your area may have conducted architectural surveys.

Old Address vs. New Address

☞ *Good for all urban and suburban homes*

As you research the past of your home, keep in mind that your home's house number and even the name of your street may have been different in the past. In fact, your home may have had several former numbers, and the name of your street could have changed more than once. Old maps, phone books, and city directories will be most useful here. (City directories are what people used before phone books were common.) When a street name or number was changed, maps and directories generally included both new and old numbers and names for a year or two after the change. Often the old number or name appears in parentheses. Look for a separate index to reference old and new street names; it's worth asking for.

Write down all former house numbers and street names of your home. These could prove invaluable when you are researching your home and find a reference to an address in the old system.

Note the names of all people listed at the address of your home in the directory or phone book. People with different surnames might have been married daughters living with the family. Other names might have been those of servants or boarders.

What Families Owned Your House?

House History Equals Homeowners' History

☞ *Good for all homes*

When you've finished looking at the deeds to your property, you'll have a list of all the owners' names. The more you discover about these people, the more you'll learn about your home. Former owners of your house, or their descendants, can provide wonderful information and stories that

Some of the best sources of fascinating and intimate details about your house can come from former owners of your home. You may find them (or their descendants) through your research, or they may find you and ring the doorbell one day when they are back in town for a wedding or funeral.

you'll never find in the public records. These people are also the best source of vintage photos of your home. Look for genealogy and family history files at libraries or historical societies.

Researching the former owners of your house is very similar to the work that genealogists do. (If you have friends who are researching their family tree, ask them for pointers on where to find information in your area.) Genealogy files can help you sort out relationships and will often supply the names of wives and children of owners. Use these names to verify, for example, that you are researching the Charles Gustafson that lived in your house and not an unrelated Charles Gustafson.

Make a list of all the families who have owned your house and the dates they bought and sold the house. This will help narrow down the time periods you're seeking for each family. For example, if someone owned your land in the 1880s, there's no use looking for their name in a file of 1960's newspaper clippings.

If you find a genealogy file or family file for a family that owned your home, make copies of as much information as you can. That way, you'll be able to refer to it throughout the research process.

Genealogy or family files sometimes list descendants or mention if someone retired to Miami or Sun City. Hint: Look for descendants' names in your local phone book. (The less common the surname, the better.) Look up the phone numbers of out-of-state people on the Internet.

"...for some intimate accounts of what has gone on inside your particular four walls, try to locate any former owners or occupants or their relatives. Neighbors should be of help here, and might themselves provide some good stories."

THIS OLD HOUSE

INDIANAPOLIS-MARION COUNTY PUBLIC LIBRARY

Klondike or Bust!

While researching an 1895 house, I discovered that the first owners did not pay off their mortgage and lost the home to foreclosure in 1898. When I examined the court papers, I discovered that when the summons was supposed to have been delivered to the man of the house, he could not be reached because he was in the Klondike area of the Alaskan Territory.

Putting two and two together, I realized that he must have gone there for the Klondike Gold Rush. He didn't find gold and the lender foreclosed on the house and it was sold at auction.

This was confirmed when I found the family in the 1900 census. They were living with relatives in a rental house. The husband was unemployed and his occupation was listed as "prospector."

Where and How to Find Deeds for Your House

☞ *Good for all homes*

Deeds are one of the best sources of information about the history of your house (phone books and obituaries are the other two), but finding deeds can be one of the most challenging parts of your research. If you have more money than time, you can pay a title company to do the research. Tell them that you want copies of all the deeds for your property.

Before you head out on your search for deeds, look through any documents that you have saved from the closing on your house. There may be some items that provide clues to the history of your home. If you're lucky, a former owner might have left an "abstract of title" (also called a "property abstract") for your property. This would contain the names of past owners of your property. Title abstracts were used up through the early decades of the 20th century before title insurance was widely used.

Depending on the system of indexing that is used in your area, deeds may have individual numbers, book and page numbers, or book and volume and page numbers. (Pages are sometimes referred to as "folios.")

There are two main systems of indexing deeds:

1. By the names of the grantors (sellers) and grantees (buyers). (In some areas, the grantor index is called the "direct index," and the grantee index is called the "indirect index" or "reverse index.")

2. By tract (all the deeds for one small area are grouped together)

A few areas use other methods of indexing deeds. Ask about written information detailing how to use the method specific to your area. Don't be afraid to ask the clerks in the office for help.

Deeds are found in government offices that may be called "Recorder of Deeds Office," "Register of Deeds," "Office of the Clerk of the Superior Court," "Registrar of Conveyances," or "Probate Department." Try looking for older deeds in your state archives if you cannot find them locally.

Not all deeds were recorded. They do not have to be. If a deed was not recorded, you will not find it in the deeds office, and there will be a gap in your title chain. (See the section "Chaining the Title" on page 108). You probably will never find a missing deed. Deeds that convey property from one family member to another, or from one close acquaintance to another, are the types of deeds that are most likely to have never been recorded. I guess the seller and buyer figured that they knew who owned the property and it wasn't anyone else's business.

Large groups of deeds may also be missing because they were destroyed by a flood or fire, or simply lost. If this is the case in your area, you'll have to rely on other sources of information such as censuses, city directories, phone books, land-ownership maps (for rural areas), and bird's-eye-view maps (for urban areas). There are sections in this book for each of these sources.

It's a good idea to trace property owners' names backwards through the grantee index and forward through the grantor index, because sometimes a property transaction will appear in only one index.

Tell the clerks in the deeds office that you are looking for all the past deeds connected to your property. Don't be afraid to ask for help!

"Make sure you have the right house! More than once a researcher has mistaken the plat and lot numbers, deed book references, or tax ledger information and proceeded carefully to research the wrong house."

UNCOVERING THE HISTORY OF YOUR HOUSE

RHODE ISLAND HISTORICAL SOCIETY

A Deed Does Not Equal a House

I once researched a house that a developer wanted to move or tear down. Someone had found an 1850's deed, and had mistakenly assumed that the house must have been built in the 1850s because there was a deed. The property owner in the 1850s was the man who founded the town, and this novice researcher then leapt to the conclusion that the house was built in the 1850s by the founder of the town.

I was asked to research the house to make sure that this was so, but sadly, I could tell just from looking at the house that it wasn't that old. And sure enough, it wasn't. The man who owned the property in the 1850s had owned most of the land in that area. From the prices on the deeds, I found that the house was built in the late 1880s or early 1890s. Sadly, the house was torn down. That's one of the few times that I felt bad about doing a house history.

"Chaining the Title"

☞ *Good for all homes*

Start with your current deed, the one *you* signed when you bought your home. That deed contains your name (and perhaps your spouse's) and the seller's name. The seller's name is generally listed first on a deed and is called the "grantor." Your name, the buyer or "grantee," is listed second. From this deed, you know the name of the person who sold you the home. Next, you want to find the previous deed.

On the previous deed, the person who sold you the home was the buyer or "grantee." And the person who sold them the land was listed as "grantor." Connecting deeds where a person is the seller

As you find the deeds for your property, arrange them in chronological order to see how the property passed from one set of owners to the next.

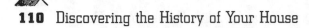

(grantor) on one deed and the buyer (grantee) on the previous deed is called "chaining the title."

If all the deeds for your property have been recorded, you should be able to chain the title back

as far as you wish. Sometimes, however, a deed
may never have been recorded, so you will not be

able to find it. If this is the case, try looking for the mortgage in the index books. If that is not there either, you will have to glean the information about urban and suburban homes from phone books or city directories, and use land-ownership maps to help sort out owners for homes in rural areas.

"... you should always keep in mind the possibility that the record that you need to complete your research may simply not be available. Many documents were lost or otherwise strayed from the official repositories that one would expect to find them in."

HOW TO RESEARCH THE HISTORY OF YOUR HOUSE
(OR OTHER BUILDING) IN NEW ORLEANS

WAYNE M. EVERARD

What You *Won't* Find on a Deed

☛ *Good for all homes*

The purpose of a deed is to show who owns a particular piece of *land*. The key word here is "land." Deeds are concerned with *land*, not *houses*. It's a rare deed that mentions anything about the existence of a house. If you find such a deed for your property, treasure it.

Most deeds do not mention structures on the property. Usually you have to use the price of the property as a guide to whether it is vacant or not.

Understanding Types of Deeds

☞ *Good for all homes*

You'll probably encounter plenty of abbreviations as you search through deeds and mortgage indexes. Here are some of the more common abbreviations and my definitions:

Agt – Agreement; a contract between the grantor (seller) and the grantee (buyer). Look at all agreements involving your property; they may contain information about the architect of your house, the price, etc.

Agmt – Same as Agt. (see above)

D – Deed; a legal instrument (document) that transfers property from the grantor (seller) to the grantee (buyer), but does not contain a warranty (guarantee) that the grantor owns the property. For your research, there is little difference between a deed and a warranty deed. Both transfer property from one owner to another.

DT – Deed of Trust (also called "Trust Deed"); this is similar to a mortgage. Trust deeds were used more often in the past, and can be confusing because they look like deeds or warranty deeds. A trust deed does not generally mean that the property changed hands. In a trust deed, the grantor (in this case, the property owner) gives the title to the property to the grantee (in this case, the person lending the money) until the grantor (property owner) pays back the loan in full.

ML – Mechanic's Lien; if a tradesperson works on a home and is not paid in full, he or she can file a mechanic's lien so that when the property owner sells the property, the tradesperson will be paid off at the closing. The name of the company filing the lien can sometimes indicate what type of work was done on the house. If you're lucky enough to find the actual mechanic's lien itself, it could provide very specific information about the work done on your house.

Mtg – Mortgage; the grantor (property owner) gives a mortgage (a promise to repay money) to the grantee (lending institution). This can be a little confusing because we often say "I got a mortgage . . .", but actually homeowners *give* a mortgage to a lending institution when they receive money. Mortgages don't usually give you any more information about a house than you would get on a deed, but you might look at mortgages on your property if you are not getting much information from the deeds.

Pat – Patent; also called a land grant. This is often found when the United States Government sells or gives away the land to homesteaders for the first time after it is surveyed. This would apply to areas surveyed after the Revolutionary War. Patents were sometimes given to veterans as payment for their service.

QC – Same as QCD (see below).

QCD – Quit Claim Deed; in this type of deed, the grantor gives up all claims to a piece of property to the grantee. Sometimes a quit claim deed transfers ownership of property from one owner to another, but other times a property owner will ask for a quit claim deed from someone in the area who owns a lot of property just to make sure that that person will not try to claim ownership to the land in the future.

Rel – Release; the grantor (lending institution) gives a release to a grantee (property owner who previously borrowed money from the grantor) stating that the money has been paid in full. Releases do not usually provide much useful information.

SD – Sheriff's Deed; often used to convey property at an auction to the highest bidder, usually for non-payment of taxes. A sheriff's deed can transfer property from one owner to another. However the former owner can sometimes take a year or two to repay the back taxes, pay a penalty, and reclaim his or her property.

TD – Trust Deed (also called "Deed of Trust"); this is similar to a mortgage. Trust deeds were used more often in the past, and can be confusing because they look like deeds or warranty deeds. I have known people to go off on all kinds of tangents thinking that the grantee on the trust deed was the new owner. This would only happen if the grantor defaulted on the loan. A trust deed does not generally mean that the property changed hands. In a trust deed, the grantor (in this case, the property owner) gives the title to the property to the grantee (in this case, the person lending the money) until the grantor (property owners) pays back the loan in full.

WD – Warranty Deed; the grantor (seller) transfers property (along with a guarantee that he or she really owns that property) to the grantee (buyer). This is the most common form of property transfer. Most of the documents that you look at will be warranty deeds.

Ask the clerks at the deed office about any other abbreviations you find. They might have some printed material about abbreviations.

> # *Signed with an X*
>
> *Every so often, I come across a deed from the 1800s that is signed with an X. The signer made a large X on the signature line, and then someone else — probably a notary public — wrote in parentheses (his mark).*
>
> *When you find a document signed like this, do not assume that the signer was illiterate. Reading and writing were often taught as two separate subjects in the 1700s and 1800s, so many people could read, but never learned to write.*

Squeezing Information from a Deed

☞ *Good for all homes*

Whenever you locate a deed for your property, it's a good idea to make a copy for your house history file. Then you can examine the deed carefully and refer back to it later if you wish. When you get a copy of a deed, make sure that you have all the pages. Deeds can be very short (less than one page), or they can be several pages long. Having a copy of a deed will also enable you to enlarge it on a photocopier to make it easier to read.

Whenever you locate a deed for your property, it's a good idea to check the deeds that were recorded on the pages before and after. Sometimes these deeds also relate to your property.

Most deeds follow a similar format and contain the same types of information. Since deeds form the foundation for much of your house history research, look at them carefully. There's a lot of information in a deed, as well as the information between the lines.

Here is a list of the various parts of the deed in the order that they appear on most deeds. You can squeeze a lot of information out of a deed if you examine it carefully.

Type of document – Documents may also be called "instruments." Often the type of document is printed at the very top of a deed. This is especially true of deeds in the second half of the 1800s and those that were written on fill-in-the-blank forms. Most deeds that you look at will simply be called "deeds" or "warranty deeds." (See the glossary on page 271 to learn more about these terms.)

Deed number – In some areas of the country, every deed has a unique number. The format varies from area to area, but it's usually a number at least five digits long.

Index number/s – Deeds generally have an index number that indicates the number of the book (also called "volume") and the number of the page (also called "folio") on which the deed was copied. Sometimes this is written with a slash separating the book and page numbers, such as "456/34." Ask about this when you are in the office where deeds are filed.

Grantors' names – The grantors are the sellers, and grantors' information is always listed first on a deed. Look at the name/s carefully. This is often the only time that you see the wife's name or middle names spelled out. Generally the husband's name comes first, but not always. If the wife's name comes first, this could mean that the property was hers. Beware – mistakes can occur on deeds, and I have seen names misspelled on deeds.

Grantors' marital status – If the grantors are married, the deed will say something like "husband and wife" or "and his wife." If a man and woman are listed, and the deed does not say this, the two people could be related or may simply be business partners. If the man and woman listed on the deed are not husband and wife, but share the same surname, they may be a brother and sister who inherited the property from their parents.

Grantors' address – Generally only the town or township and state are listed. If you're *really* lucky, you might find a street address written here.

If the grantors live in another town, check with the historical society in *that* town for information about them. You might find more information about them outside your town. For example, if the grantors lived in your home when they were newlyweds and their children were young, there might be more information about them in the next town in which they lived when the children were older and the parents had more time for community involvement. Check these people's names on the previous deed when those people were the grantees (buyers). If the people were living in another town or city when they *bought* your property, and lived in that town or city when they *sold* your property, they may never have lived in your home.

Grantees' names – These are the buyers' names. As with the grantors' names, look at these names carefully. There is usually less information about grantees than grantors in deeds. Often the wife's name is not listed.

Grantees' address – Note this carefully. If the grantees are not listed as living in your city or town, it may be that they had not moved into the house yet. Check this with the succeeding deed for the property, when these same people are the grantors. If they are *still* living outside your area, they may not have lived in your house. Check with the historical society in their place of residence to see if there is any information about them. If the people spent the active, productive part of their lives elsewhere and moved to your home when they retired, there could be more information about them in their previous town.

Consideration – This is usually the amount of money that changed hands. Note the price and compare it to the price on the previous and subsequent deeds for the property. Usually a huge jump in price for the same piece of property indicates that a house has been built. Consideration is not always money, sometimes it is property or other items of value. Occasionally you see a heart-warming phrase such as "for $1 and the love of parents for their son." This (obviously) indicates the family relationship between grantors and grantees. Around the early 1900s, only a nominal sum of $1 or $10 began to be written on some deeds in place of the actual price.

Property description – The legal description of the property that is changing hands appears here. If the property has been subdivided, the description might read something like "lot 30 on block 2 of Glen Park Estates." If the property has not been subdivided, the description might be something like "the eastern 1/2 of the northeast 1/4 of 34-12-9." Or it might be an extremely complicated description such as "Commencing at a stake at the south side of a red oak stump, thence 17 degrees NE 22 chains and 21 links . . ." (If you're trying to untangle a description like this one, see the sections "N 18.5 Degrees 3 Chains 5 Links" and "North 15 Degrees East 13 Chains, East 8 Chains . . ." on pages 184–185.) Look at the description on the deed carefully to make sure that the deed includes the property you are researching. As you go back in time, you will probably find that your property was once part of a larger piece of property such as a farm or estate. Researching the owners of this larger parcel will give you an idea of how the land was used before your house appeared on it.

Restrictions, etc. – Sometimes you'll find other information written on the deed. Look carefully at anything that you find. You may find a description that says, "said property was formerly the Ben Smith farm." This could be an important clue that will help you in your hunt for information. Any references to wills should also be checked out. (See the section "Where There's a Will, There's Information" on page 173.) Sometimes there are restrictions on the race or religion of the property buyers. Some restrictions reflect the sellers' desire to protect property values. These include the minimum price of house that can be built on the lot, or a ban on commercial activities, chicken and pig farms, or the sale of alcohol.

Grantors' signatures – It's easy to overlook the rest of the information on a deed, but don't stop now. As you look at the signatures, try to figure out if the handwriting is different from that in the rest of the document. If the handwriting appears to be the same in the signatures *and* the body of the document, the clerk who copied the deed also copied the signatures. If the handwriting in the signatures is clearly *different* from that in the rest of the document, the grantors were present when the document was recorded and actually signed the copy. If so, look at the signatures carefully. These are probably the ultimate source for the correct spelling of names. This is very useful for names that appear as *McDonald* in half the information you've discovered, and *MacDonald* in the other half. The people signing their names are the best sources for correct spelling. Obviously this does not work when people signed their name with an X, as sometimes happened.

Grantees' signatures – As with the grantors' signatures, look at the handwriting and check the spelling of the names.

Document signature date – Every deed that is recorded (or filed) in the deeds office should have two dates: the date that the deed was signed, and the date that the deed was recorded (copied in the deeds office). The *earlier* date is the most important date for your research. This date is the date of closing – the date that the property actually changed hands.

Document recording date – This date, usually a week or two later than the signature date, is the date that the deed was brought to the deeds office to be copied, filed, or recorded. When a deed was brought into the office (before the age of photo-copiers and computers), a clerk copied the deed onto the next blank page in the record book. Deeds are generally recorded in chronological order *according to the date that they were brought into the office.* Deeds can be recorded years, and even decades, after they have been signed. This means that an 1840's deed that was brought into the recording office in the 1920s was recorded amongst the 1920's deeds. The earlier date on the deed was the date that the property changed hands, however. The fact that the deed was recorded 80 years after it was signed is interesting, but it does not affect the date of the property transfer.

Anything else – Look carefully at any other information that you find on a deed. Sometimes there is a reference to a will or a court case. If you find this, try to find those other documents (ask the clerks in the deeds office for help). If you're very lucky, you may find a reference to the previous deed with which the grantor (seller) acquired the property. If so, this will greatly facilitate your search backward through the owners.

"It's surprising how often a 'meaningless' fact gleaned from one source may dovetail with a tidbit picked up elsewhere and produce an important clue."

HOUSE DETECTIVE: GUIDE TO
RESEARCHING BIRMINGHAM BUILDINGS

ANN MCCORQUODALE BURKHARDT

Does "Pfingste" Sound Like "Kingston" to You?

I was once tracing the ownership of a piece of property back in time. The person who sold the piece of property was named Kingston, according to the deed. So, I looked for a deed in the grantee index in which Mr. Kingston had bought the property. I looked and looked and looked.

That night, after I got home, I realized that in one place on the deed, the name Kingston almost looked as if it had been written "Pfingston." That was all I had to go on, but I went back to the Recorder of Deeds Office and looked for "Pfingston." Couldn't find that either. By this

> *time, I was fairly familiar with all the names in the PF list, and I noticed that there was a surname "Pfingste." So I looked under that name, and finally found the person I was looking for. Apparently someone had written the name Pfingste as Kingston!*

Using the Document Information Forms

☞ *Good for all homes*

Use the form on the following page to help you extract all the useful information from a deed. A deed is like a snapshot in time. Copy and enlarge the form and fill out one for each deed. When you're done, lay your document information forms in chronological order (according to signature dates) to see the progression of activity for your property.

Document/instrument # _____

Book & page # _____

Type of document _____

Grantor/s (seller/s) name/s_____

Grantor/s (seller/s) marital status_____

Grantor/s (seller/s) address_____

Grantee/s (buyer/s) name/s_____

Grantee/s (buyer/s) marital status_____

Grantee/s (buyer/s) address_____

Consideration ($) _____

Lot/s or property description _____

_____

Any restrictions_____

Grantor/s (seller/s) signatures_____

Grantee/s (buyer/s) signatures _____

Date document was signed _____

Date document was recorded _____

Anything else _____

Name Misspellings Can Drive You Knutz

People seemed to be more laid back about the spelling of names before 1900. "Pride in diversity" was not necessarily the common belief at that time either. In fact, there were some very strong anti-immigrant feelings. As such, ethnic surnames were frequently misspelled.

I once came across a German surname: Moench. In a file on the family, a local genealogist had noted that there were six spellings of the name: Mong, Monch, Munch, Moonch, Moeng, and Ming!

Other times, immigrants' names were Anglicized. The German surname Klein became Little, Fischer became Fisher, and Friedrich Graue became Fred Gray. I sometimes wonder how many of these changes were done with the immigrants' permission, and how many of these transformations were forced upon people.

Deciphering Old-Style Script

☛ *Good for all homes*

The older the deeds are, the harder they are to read. In the late 1800s, many documents were pre-printed forms, and the lawyers or clerks filled in the blanks. In the mid-1800s and earlier, most documents were completely handwritten. Sometimes the handwriting is beautiful, but often it is just awful. I guess the records clerk was chosen for his political connections rather than the clarity of his handwriting.

When you go back to 1800's documents, you often find "Spenser" or "Copperplate" script. This style of script was a lot more elaborate than the styles we use today. There were lots of curlicues on the letters, and when you look through page after page of this stuff on microfilm, it's really hard on your eyes.

If you will be dealing with a lot of documents written in this old-style script, it might be worth your while to look for calligraphy books in bookstores or libraries that show the various ways people formed their letters. This might help you decipher some of the handwriting that you encounter in your research.

No Saloons or Asylums, Please

Old deeds sometimes have restrictions about land use and what kind of people can live on the property. One 1890's deed I found stipulated that, "said premises shall be used for residence purposes only and shall not be used or built upon in any manner or for any purpose tending to render the same injurious or offensive to a residence neighborhood . . . no saloon shall be kept or permitted to be kept or liquor sold or permitted to be sold upon any part of said premises."

A 1912 home that I researched had a deed that stated, "no intoxicating liquors, malt, vinous or spirituous, shall ever be bargained or sold upon said premises." The deed also forbade chicken and pig farms, and stated that the property could not be used "for the purposes of a public or private hospital, asylum or other institution for the treatment or instruction of the diseased, the defective or dependent." When I see something like this in a deed, my guess is that the person selling the property lived nearby and did not want odors or inmates wafting about the neighborhood.

Your Home May Have Been Rented

☞ *Good for all homes*

Don't assume that the family who owned your home actually lived there. Just because someone's name is on a deed does not mean that she or he lived in the home. If the buyers ("grantees") did not live in your city or town when they bought your home, and did not live in your area when the home was sold, they may not have lived in your home at all. Your home might have been occupied by tenants.

Look at phone books of that time period to see if the owner was listed at your address.

Slightly more than two-thirds of Americans now own their own homes, but before the post World War II building boom, only about one-half of Americans owned their homes. So, about half of the population lived in apartments or rented houses. (There were fewer townhouses and condominiums in the past than there are today.) So, keep in mind that tenants may have lived in your home at some point in the past.

———

"Do not just ask for 'old pictures of the house,' but look at any family photos during the time the family lived in the house."
DOCUMENTING A HISTORIC STRUCTURE IN ATLANTA
KENNETH H. THOMAS, JR.

Investigating Owners to Learn Even More

Let Your Fingers Do the Walking

☞ *Good for homes built before 1950*

One of the best sources of information about the people who lived in your house are old phone books and city directories. You know what a phone book is; a city directory looks just like a phone book without phone numbers. City directories originated before the telephone was invented.

You'll find old phone books and city directories at historical societies and libraries. They can date back more than 150 years. The early directories contained an alphabetical list of residents and their addresses, and sometimes listed people's occupations. There were no telephones yet, so there were no phone numbers.

Look up the names of all the previous owners of your home during the years that they owned your home. The first year that an owner is listed at your address might indicate the construction date of your home. Remember that the information contained in phone books was usually gathered the year before the phone book was published.

Early phone books were patterned after city directories. They also listed people's names, occupations, the name of their employer, and sometimes wives and children's names. This extra information disappeared from most phone books by the 1930s.

In some city directories and phone books, there is a street directory. The names of the area's citizens were listed by street name and by house number. This is one way to find out if the homeowner occupied your home or if it was rented.

One 1920's phone book that I saw stated:

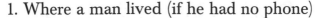

1. Where a man lived (if he had no phone)
2. Where he worked
3. What his occupation was
4. What his wife's name was
5. If he owned his own home
6. If he was a renter
7. Where a certain street was located
8. Who lived at any number on any street
[And so on all the way up to number 18!]

If the person who owned your home also owned a business, check the part of the phone book that listed businesses. You might find that the business address was the same as the residential address, and so learn that your home also served as a flower shop or a wagon manufacturing shop. This might help to explain why your home has more than one main entrance.

Keep in mind that your home may have had one or more different house numbers in the past. Your street may have had other *names* in the past as well. City and phone directories (as well as old maps) are the best sources of old street names and house numbers. Often those printed at the time of the change contained the new names and numbers and included the old names or numbers in parentheses. Sometimes there was an index in the phone book or directory that cross-indexed new and old names or numbers.

Census Records Yield Fascinating Details

☞ *Good for all homes built before 1930*

The Federal census was taken every ten years by census takers who walked up and down rural roads and the streets of cities and towns in the United States. The information that they recorded varied from one census to the next, but most census forms listed the names and ages of all family members, as well as their occupations and ethnic backgrounds. There are phonetic "Soundex" indices to censuses from 1880 to 1930. (The 1930 census is only partly indexed.) A number of states also conducted their own censuses. Ask about these at libraries and archives.

Ask your local library or historical society if they have copies of the census records for your area. If not, the National Archives and Records Administration (NARA) regional branches have nearly all the census records that you might need. Note that the census for 1880 only included families with school-aged children; most of the 1890 census records were destroyed in a fire in Washington, D.C.; and the most recent census that is available is for 1930.

The National Archives and Records Administration is located at:

National Archives and Records Administration

700 Pennsylvania Ave., NW
Washington, DC 20408
Phone: 1-800-234-8861
E-mail: inquire@nara.gov
Web site: www.nara.gov

There are also regional branches of the National
Archives. Call or write for a listing of what kinds of
records each one has. Many also offer classes or lec-
tures that you may find helpful.

Alaska
NARA's Pacific Alaska Region (Anchorage)
654 West Third Avenue
Anchorage, Alaska 99501-2145
Telephone: 907-271-2443
E-mail: alaska.archives@nara.gov
Web: www.nara.gov/regional/anchorag.html
Fax: 907-271-2442

California
Laguna Niguel
NARA's Pacific Region (Laguna Niguel)
24000 Avila Road, First Floor – East Entrance
Laguna Niguel, California 92677-3497
Telephone: 949-360-2641
E-mail: laguna.archives@nara.gov
Web: www.nara.gov/regional/laguna.html
Fax: 949-360-2624

San Francisco (San Bruno)
NARA's Pacific Region (San Francisco)
1000 Commodore Drive
San Bruno, California 94066-2350
Telephone: 650-876-9009
E-mail: sanbruno.archives@nara.gov
Fax: 650-876-9233
Web: www.nara.gov/regional/sanfranc.html

Colorado
Denver
NARA's Rocky Mountain Region
Building 48, Denver Federal Center
West 6th Avenue and Kipling Street
Denver, Colorado 80225
P. O. Box 25307
Denver, Colorado 80225-0307
Telephone: 303-236-0804
E-mail: denver.archives@nara.gov
Web: www.nara.gov/regional/denver.html
Fax: 303-236-9297

Georgia
Atlanta (East Point)
NARA's Southeast Region
1557 St. Joseph Avenue
East Point, Georgia 30344-2593
Telephone: 404-763-7474
E-mail: atlanta.center@nara.gov

Web: www.nara.gov/regional/atlanta.html
Fax: 404-763-7815 or 404-763-7967

Illinois
Chicago
NARA's Great Lakes Region (Chicago)
7358 South Pulaski Road
Chicago, Illinois 60629-5898
Telephone: 773-581-7816
E-mail: chicago.archives@nara.gov
Web: www.nara.gov/regional/chicago.html
Fax: 312-353-1294

Maryland
College Park
Office of Regional Records Services
National Archives and Records Administration
8601 Adelphi Road
College Park, Maryland 20740-6001
Telephone: 301-713-7200
Fax: 301-713-7205

Suitland
Washington National Records Center
4205 Suitland Road
Suitland, Maryland 20746-8001
Telephone: 301-457-7000
E-mail: suitland.center@nara.gov
Web: www.nara.gov/records/wnrc.html
Fax: 301-457-7117

Massachusetts

Boston (Waltham)

NARA's Northeast Region (Boston)

380 Trapelo Road

Waltham, Massachusetts 02452-6399

Telephone: 781-647-8104

E-mail: waltham.center@nara.gov

Web: www.nara.gov/regional/boston.html

Fax: 781-647-8088

Pittsfield

NARA's Northeast Region (Pittsfield)

10 Conte Drive

Pittsfield, Massachusetts 01201-8230

Telephone: 413-445-6885

E-mail: pittsfield.archives@nara.gov

Web: www.nara.gov/regional/pittsfie.html

Fax: 413-445-7599

Missouri

Kansas City

NARA's Central Plains Region (Kansas City)

2312 East Bannister Road

Kansas City, Missouri 64131-3011

Telephone: 816-926-6272

E-mail: kansascity.archives@nara.gov

Web: www.nara.gov/regional/kansas.html

Fax: 816-926-6982

Lee's Summit

NARA's Central Plains Region (Lee's Summit)

200 Space Center Drive

Lee's Summit, Missouri 64064-1182

Telephone: 816-478-7079

E-mail: kansascitycave.center@nara.gov

Web: www.nara.gov/regional/leesumit.html

Fax: 816-478-7625

St. Louis

NARA's National Personnel Records Center

Civilian Personnel Records

111 Winnebago Street

St. Louis, Missouri 63118-4199

E-mail: cpr.center@nara.gov

Web: www.nara.gov/regional/cpr.html

Fax: 314-538-5719

New York

New York City

NARA's Northeast Region (New York City)

201 Varick Street

New York, New York 10014-4811

Telephone: 212-337-1300

E-mail: newyork.archives@nara.gov

Web: www.nara.gov/regional/newyork.html

Fax: 212-337-1306

Ohio

Dayton
NARA's Great Lakes Region (Dayton)
3150 Springboro Road
Dayton, Ohio 45439-1883
Telephone: 937-225-2852
E-mail: dayton.center@nara.gov
Web: www.nara.gov/regional/dayton.html
Fax: 937-225-7236

Pennsylvania

Philadelphia
NARA's Mid Atlantic Region (Center City
Philadelphia)
900 Market Street
Philadelphia, Pennsylvania 19107-4292
Telephone: 215-597-3000
E-mail:philadelphia.archives@nara.gov
Web: www.nara.gov/regional/philacc.html
Fax: 215-597-2303

NARA's Mid Atlantic Region (Northeast Phila-
delphia)
14700 Townsend Road
Philadelphia, Pennsylvania 19154-1096
Telephone: 215-671-9027
E-mail: philadelphia.center@nara.gov
Web: www.nara.gov/regional/philane.html
Fax: 215-671-8001

Texas

Fort Worth
NARA's Southwest Region
501 West Felix Street, Building 1
Fort Worth, Texas 76115-3405
P. O. Box 6216
Fort Worth, Texas 76115-0216
Telephone: 817-334-5525
E-mail: ftworth.archives@nara.gov
Web: www.nara.gov/regional/ftworth.html
Fax: 817-334-5621

Washington (State)

Seattle
NARA's Pacific Alaska Region (Seattle)
6125 Sand Point Way NE
Seattle, Washington 98115-7999
Telephone: 206-526-6501
E-mail: seattle.archives@nara.gov
Web: www.nara.gov/regional/seattle.html
Fax: 206-526-6575

Ask Churches About People Records

☛ *Good for all homes*

I've had some luck contacting local churches to learn about someone's death date. If your research reveals to which church a family belonged, call or write to the secretary of that church and ask about a death date. If that doesn't work, ask the secretary if there is a particular cemetery in which church members were usually buried. Then, contact that cemetery. The death date or interment (burial) date can lead you to the obituary in the local paper. Obituaries can yield information about wives, children and grandchildren (could they still be alive?), people's occupations, how long they lived in the area, etc.

"People are often the greatest resource in the research of old buildings."

SOURCES & SEARCHES: DOCUMENTING HISTORIC BUILDINGS IN NEW MEXICO

FLOYD McHUGH

Church records can provide information about homeowners who were active in the congregation — especially women, as church-related activities were more acceptable than working outside the home.

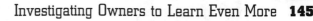

Listening to Oral Histories

☞ *Good for all homes*

Don't forget to ask about oral histories when visiting libraries and historical societies. These can contain valuable or interesting information from the *people* trail. If you're lucky, the oral histories will be indexed. If not, they can be time-consuming to wade through. Look for oral histories done by people who lived in your area. Sometimes they are on a cassette tape, while others have been transcribed.

Look at *Any* Lists of People That You Find

☞ *Good for all homes*

In some locations, you might find special censuses that were conducted to count the number of schoolchildren or there might be old voter registrations rolls available. These might confirm that a certain owner lived in your home at that time.

"Family-held photographs usually provide the richest source of visual information about the exterior and interior appearances of historic homes."

HISTORIC RESIDENCE RESEARCH RESOURCES: A GUIDE FOR THE LAYPERSON TO SOURCES OF BUILDING DATE IN FRESNO

JOHN EDWARD POWELL AND KEVIN ENNS-REMPEL

Going Once, Going Twice, Sold!

☞ *Good for all homes*

Houses, or to be more specific, the property on which they are located can be sold for back taxes if the owner is delinquent in paying taxes. Houses can also be sold at auction if the homeowner does not pay back his mortgage on schedule. A deed for a tax sale usually looks different from one in which one person sells the house (property) to another. Often the grantor (seller) has an official title such as "clerk of the court" or "sheriff." Sometimes the deed itself is called a "sheriff's deed" or "SD."

There are a couple of things to keep in mind about tax sales. One is that you may be able to find the official notice of the sale in the local newspaper. Another thing to remember is that the original owner (the one who was delinquent in paying taxes) sometimes had a year or two to buy back the property by paying the tax bill plus a penalty fee. In this case, the original owner would continue to own the property and could sell it at a later date.

"There is no way to predict what you will find until you begin."

HOW TO RESEARCH THE HISTORY OF YOUR HOME IN NEW CASTLE COUNTY, DELAWARE

SUSAN BRIZZOLARA AND VALERIE CESNA

Go to Court

☞ *Good for all homes*

If you encounter any references to court cases while researching the deeds to your property, they could be worth pursuing. The court records might contain useful or interesting information about your home or its former occupants.

Write down any dates, names, court case numbers, etc., and ask the people in the deeds office where you should go to find the records you want.

God Bless the Mormon Family History Centers

☞ *Good for all homes*

Another place to look for information about the families who lived in your house is at the Family History Centers run by the Church of Jesus Christ of the Latter-Day Saints (also called "LDS" or "Mormons"). People of the Mormon faith do genealogy research so that they can arrange to have their ancestors baptized posthumously. They very generously make their facilities available to anyone doing genealogy research. You can locate the Family History Center in your area by visiting the web site www.familysearch.org.

The main branch of the LDS genealogy library in Salt Lake City, Utah is open to the public. You

Because of privacy laws, it is sometimes harder to find out about the people who lived in your house after the 1930s. The Social Security Death Index (SSDI) indexed people who died from 1962 until the present.

can also access their catalog online and ask your local FHC to order items for you:

Family History Library

35 North West Temple St.

Salt Lake City, Utah 84150-3400

Phone: 801-240-2331

Fax: 801-240-1584

e-mail: fhl@ldschurch.org

You can search their library catalog at www.family search.org.

The information at each Family History Center varies, so be prepared to explore lots of files, microfilm, and microfiche. Personal computers may be available with files and programs useful for genealogists. Don't be afraid to ask for help. The volunteers I've encountered are all experienced genealogists themselves.

One extremely useful source of information generally available at Family History Centers is the Social Security Death Index (SSDI). This is also available at the LDS web site www.ancestry.com. (Other genealogy web sites have the SSDI as well.) This alphabetized index includes the names of people who had social security numbers and died after 1961. You can limit your search by state and by approximate year of birth. This is useful for very common names. You will often learn the month and year that a person died, and sometimes the zip code of the community to which the social security death benefits were sent. The Social Security Death

Index is one of the very few sources of information about people who lived in your home after 1930 (the year of the last census available for public inspection). Knowing the month and year that

someone died will help you look for their obituary in the local paper.

Ask About Donor Files

☞ *Good for all homes*

Some historical societies and museums keep a file on any person who ever donated anything to them. Check the list of names of all the people who have owned your home against your local historical society's list of donor names. Some institutions may be reluctant to let you look at the files. In that case, show them your list, and ask them to check if anyone on your list has donated anything.

You might find that a former owner of your home donated some photos or other interesting items. Some historical societies keep track of these people's addresses when they move away from your area. Perhaps some of these former owners are still alive and you could write to them. They are your best source of vintage photos of your home.

———

"You will likely be rewarded with a great deal of information on your home's history, its alterations, and former occupants."

RESEARCHING YOUR ILLINOIS HOUSE

GREG KOOS

ILLINOIS HISTORIC PRESERVATION AGENCY

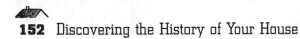

Looking for vintage photos of your home? Follow the people trail. Look for former owners or their descendants. If you're lucky, you'll find some with unusual names that you can search for in telephone listings on the Internet.

Look for Homeowners in Local History Books

☞ *Good for all homes*

After you've researched the deeds for your property, you'll have a list of all the owners' names, when they lived, and where they lived. Look for these names in the indexes of local history books in your local library or historical society. Perhaps you'll discover that a former owner was active in your local government or was a founding member of a church. If you're really lucky, you might even find a photo of a former owner standing in front of your house.

Deeds will also tell you where the owners of your property lived when they bought your property, and where they lived when they sold it. If the owners lived in another community at one point, consider contacting *that* area's library and historical society to see if the owners of your property were mentioned in *their* history books.

Search for Vintage *Who's Who* Books

☞ *Good for all homes built after 1890*

Ask at libraries and historical societies for vintage *Who's Who*-type books. Look to see if any of the people who owned your home are listed. You'll find information about the person's accomplishments, spouse and children (could they still be alive?), etc.

Businessmen and prominent professional men people the pages of vintage Who's Who-*type books. Look in these books for the names of former owners of your home.*

Many libraries keep books and other materials pertaining to local history in a special area or room called "Local History," "Genealogy," or "Special Collections." Ask about this if you don't find what you're looking for on the regular bookshelves.

Don't Overlook Old Newspapers

☛ *Good for all homes*

Look for old newspapers (probably on microfilm) at local libraries or historical societies. Most local papers are not indexed, but a few are, so it's worth asking about an index.

You might be able to find a real estate ad for your house. If you've researched the deeds for your property, you know the closing date (the earlier date that appears on the deed), so look at ads in local papers several months prior to this date. If you're looking in the 1960s or later, you might find a photo.

Vintage issues of local papers will also contain society columns that might have mentioned your home being built or families moving into or out of your home. Some local newspapers also printed house plans. These included a sketch of the home and floor plan along with information about how to send away for the plans. It's possible that homes in your community – yours maybe? – were built using these plans.

Local papers contain obituaries which can be extremely informative. Obits have useful information about the deceased as well as mention of survivors (could they still be living in your community?)

If you know the approximate year that your house was built, you might enjoy reading through the local papers of that time period to see what life was like for the first occupants of your home. You'll see ads for fashions, cars, household appliances, and furnishings, etc. If nothing else, you'll find the prices amusing.

Check the December and January issues of local papers. At the beginning or end of the year, some papers published real estate transactions, building permits issued, or deaths from the previous year. The times of these special issues varied. In some areas, an annual report in the newspaper called *Brick and Mortar* listed all the building permits issued in the previous 12 months. Some local papers periodically printed property sales.

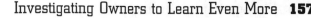

Social Directories Tell You Who Was Who

☞ *Good for urban and suburban homes*

If you think that your home might have been occupied by a prominent family, look for old copies of social directories or registers (also called "Blue Books") in libraries and historical societies. Like city directories and phone books, these listed a person's address and occupation, and sometimes listed the clubs to which they belonged. You probably won't learn much about your house, but you will learn more about the people who lived in it.

Newspapers Contain Interesting Tidbits

☞ *Good for urban and suburban homes*

Check at your local library or historical society for clippings from newspapers, usually organized under various headings. (Sometimes clippings files are called "vertical files".) Look for headings such as "history," "houses," "neighborhoods," "subdivisions," and "people's names." Check to see if there are separate files for any of your home's former owners.

If your home was formerly a store, school, tea room, etc. check for any files related to these organizations or businesses.

If you've researched the deeds to your property, you know the closing dates when your home changed hands. Sometimes the local newspaper's society column contained information about families moving into or out of town. There might be a mention of a local contractor or architect who was building your house.

Seasick Researchers

It's possible to get seasick from looking at microfilm text scrolling past on the screen minute after minute. Pretty soon the entire room seems to be moving up and down. The remedy for microfilm mal-de-mer *is the same as on a boat — stare at a distant object that is stationary. I once met a genealogist who swore that she avoided nausea by opening and closing her eyes rhythmically as the microfilm scrolled by on the screen. I've never been able to do this successfully, however.*

Farmer's Directories Left Nothing Out

☞ *Good for rural homes*

Out in the country, there were farmer's directories instead of city directories or phone books. These were similar to phone books, but they also included information such as the total acreage that the farmer owned, the name of the farm, what kind of farm it was, as well as the brand of car or truck that the family owned.

"Old houses present us with a very immediate, tangible link to local history."
UNCOVERING THE HISTORY OF YOUR HOUSE
RHODE ISLAND HISTORICAL SOCIETY

Contacting Former Owners of Your Home

☞ *Good for all homes*

Former owners (and their descendants) can be wonderful sources of information about your home. People who have lived in your home can tell you things about it that you will never find in public records. These people are also the best source of vintage photos of your home.

APR · 55

Was (or is) your home a farmhouse? Look for owners' names in farmer's directories which were very similar to phone books and city directories.

Approach former owners with care, however. Some people may be afraid that you are contacting them to complain (or file a lawsuit) because the cistern under the backyard collapsed and the dog fell in, or someone got an electrical shock because the wiring was done improperly.

I advise writing a letter, waiting a week, and then following up with a phone call. I usually try to send the people some information that I've uncovered about the house or their family. Including a recent photo of the home to jog their memory might also be a good idea.

In your letter, be sure to stress that you love your old house, they don't build 'em like they used to, etc. Tell the former owner that you would love to have a copy of an old photo of the house and offer to pay for the cost of making a copy.

You might also tell the former homeowners that you would love to have them drop by for a visit. If they accept, they'll probably remember things about the house that they might not have remembered otherwise.

The next section features a sample letter that you can use to contact a former owner of your home. After that I've included a sample questionnaire; feel free to adapt both of these according to your particular situation.

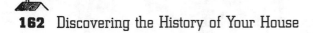

Sample Letter to the Former Owner of Your Home

Dear _____,

I am the current owner of the home at ADDRESS. I think it's a great old house, and I have recently started researching its history. I believe that you used to live in this home. Some of the other owners of this home have been: LIST THEM.

I thought you might enjoy some of the things I've discovered about the home in my research, such as: LIST A FEW THINGS.

Do you have any favorite memories or stories about living in this home? I'd love to hear about them! I would also really love to find some old photos of the home and the people who have lived here (I'd be happy to pay for the cost of copying any photos).

If you would ever like to come back and visit and see the inside of the home, please give me a call at YOUR PHONE NUMBER. I'd be happy to show you around!

I look forward to hearing from you. I have enclosed a stamped, self-addressed envelope for your convenience.

Sincerely,

P.S.–I've enclosed a photo of the way the house looks now. I thought you might find it interesting!

Sample Questionnaire for the Former Owner of Your Home

What years did you live in the house?

Did other relatives or boarders live in the house? What were their names and what bedrooms did they occupy?

What did you like best about the house?

Do you remember the names of any families that lived in the house before you did?

Did any former owners or residents ever visit the house?

Did they tell you anything about the home's history?

Did you ever find anything from former owners either in the house or out in the yard?

Do you have any photos of the house or of people who lived in it?

Do you know of anyone else who might have old photos?

Were any changes made to the house while you lived here?

How many bathrooms did the house have when you lived here?

What appliances were in the kitchen?

How was the home heated?

Did the neighborhood change while you lived in the house?

Were there any ghosts?

Was anyone born in the house?

Have you seen the house recently?

How has the house changed since you lived here?

How has the landscaping changed?

Was the yard or property a different size when you lived here?

Is there anyone in the area who might remember what the house was like years ago?

Were there ever any structures on the property such as barns, carriage houses, outhouses, etc?

Are there any memorable events (weddings, parties, etc.) that occurred while you were in the house?

Do you have photos of these events?

Ghostly Faces at the Windows

When I researched a large 1890's Queen Anne house, I managed to track down a woman who had lived in the home in the 1960s. While I was talking to her about the home's history, she asked, "Do the current owners know about the ghosts?"

I told her that, if they did, they hadn't mentioned it to me. She said that when her family had moved into the home, the previous residents had been a group of Catholic nuns. She said that the nuns told her about the ghosts whose faces showed up at the windows when the nuns pulled into the driveway. When the nuns entered the house, there was no one there. This owner said that her family also saw the ghosts.

Apparently the apparitions didn't bother the new family at first, but eventually the owner decided she wasn't comfortable sharing her home with the ghosts. She went up to the third floor, where she "felt" the ghosts most strongly, and had a "conversation" with them. She asked the ghosts to move to the large carriage house in the back of the property. She said that the ghosts must have done so, because she never saw them after that.

Clues From Beyond the Grave

Death Indexes
Lead to Obituaries

☞ *Good for all homes*

Death indexes are generally kept by the state, county, or city. I have found them in libraries or historical societies. Death dates can lead you to obituary notices in newspapers, which can provide a wealth of information about a person, his/her livelihood, and descendants. The information in an obit often answers questions that have popped up during your research.

Other sources for death dates are cemetery indexes, newspaper indexes, Vital Records Departments, and the records of funeral homes.

Take everything with a grain of salt – whether it's a story you hear from a neighbor about your house or an official legal document – any and all of these can contain errors. Check and crosscheck all information.

A Ghost Named Julia

When I researched the history of an early 1900's home, I discovered that it had been built by an elderly widow named Julia. From her obituary, I learned that she had died in the house in 1915.

I didn't know if the homeowner wanted this piece of information in the house history, so I first spoke to her about Julia. As I was telling the owner, she suddenly sat up straight. I immediately cursed myself inwardly for having told the owner something unsettling. "I have felt a presence in the house," she told me. "I've felt a female presence, not unfriendly. My cats have reacted, too. Now I know her name. Thank you!" I breathed a big sigh of relief.

Cemetery Indexes
Help You Find Obits

☞ *Good for all homes*

Look for cemetery indexes and listings at local libraries, historical societies, genealogy groups, churches, city halls, courthouses, and at the cemeteries themselves. Some cemeteries will search their records over the phone, some let you come in and look at their lists, and others want a written request and charge a fee.

Local genealogy groups and the D.A.R. (Daughters of the American Revolution) sometimes create alphabetical lists of people buried in local cemeteries. If you find the burial record of someone who owned your home, you might learn the names of spouses and children as well as the burial date (date of interment). This will help you find a person's obituary in the local newspaper.

Obits are one of the most useful sources of information about a person. They provide the names of family members (some of whom may still be living) as well as the occupation and achievements of the deceased. If you're lucky, an obit might mention when a family built their home in your area.

If you find someone in a cemetery index, it might be worth the time to visit the grave itself. You might learn something about the names of other family members. Be sure to get detailed directions

The records held by cemeteries can lead to information about death dates that can aid in finding obituaries in the local paper. Visiting the actual headstone and examining information on other related headstones can provide information about other family members.

from the cemetery staff about finding the headstone you want. Cemeteries are often not arranged alphabetically or chronologically.

Funeral Homes Can Be Helpful

☞ *Good for all homes*

In a small town, contact funeral homes that have been in existence for a long time. Ask if they have any death dates or burial dates for people who lived in your home. Death dates will give you a good idea of what dates to look up in your local newspaper to find obituaries. Obits often list the names of a surviving spouse and children (perhaps they are still alive?), and mention a person's accomplishments or occupation.

When funeral homes question why I'm asking for death dates, I usually say that I'm doing genealogy research. It seems to satisfy any reservations they might have about releasing such information.

Obituaries are Marvelous!

☞ *Good for all homes*

Obituaries are one of the three best sources of information about the people who lived in your house. (The other two best sources are deeds and old phone books.) Obituaries in the late 1800s and early 1900s waxed long and lyrical in great detail about the attributes of the deceased. These obituaries sometimes provide such information as when the person moved to the town, his or her occupation, the names of parents, spouse, and children (might some of them still be alive?). Try looking them up in a nationwide residential phone listing on the Internet.

Most obits are not indexed, but it's worth asking if there is an obituary index to papers in your area. If there is none, see the sections titled "Death Indexes Lead to Obituaries" (page 167) and "Cemetery Indexes Help You Find Obits" (page 169).

Obituary Information Solves Puzzle

I researched the tax assessor's records year by year for a house built in the 1890s, and was puzzled because the value rose steadily over a period of three years. (Normally the value jumps considerably from one year to the next when a house is built on the property.) The puzzle was solved when I found the first homeowner's obituary. He was a carpenter. He probably built the home himself little by little over several years.

Where There's a Will, There's Information

☞ Good for all homes

A Probate Court (also called "Will Records Office" or "Register of Wills") can provide useful information about the family who lived in your house. Wills are sometimes indexed by surname, date of death, or date of filing. (These records are sometimes called "estate files.")

Look carefully though any wills and associated papers that you find with wills. Generally the deceased's date of death is mentioned. This can help you find an obituary. Estate records often provide an inventory of property owned by the deceased. I've seen descriptions such as "the two-story brick house at 2345 Center Street." The contents of the home are also often inventoried and an estimate of the value of each item is given.

Wills often contain testimonials given by survivors that contain valuable information about the deceased, how many wives and children he had, etc.

A Wealth of Information in Wills

I love to read the inventories in wills. I researched an 1860's home that was owned by a judge. When he died in 1908, the furniture in the house included a black walnut bedroom set valued at $25, (imagine what antique shops would charge for this today!), a kitchen range ($2), a four-piece set of parlor furniture ($25), a marble-top table (anybody who was anybody in the late 1800s had to have a marble-top table in the parlor – value $2), and a hair mattress (stuffed with animal hair, I guess – $2).

An 1880 inventory of a farm revealed possessions that included a wolf skin robe valued at $5, a sewing machine ($4), a marble-top table (what did I tell you? – $5), 25 yards of carpet valued at $3.12 (how they came up with that odd amount I'll never know). The most curious item was a "zinc" valued at $3. My best guess is that this is a sink or bathtub, lined with zinc.

The testimonial given as part of another will included the information that both the deceased and his oldest son had the same name. No other documents mentioned them as father and son, or senior and junior. This cleared up a lot of confusion for me because I found the same name on deeds dating from the Civil War up through the 1920s, and I was trying to figure out how old this guy could be!

Curious About the History of Your Land?

Going Back to the Beginning of History

☛ *Good for all homes*

    If you are interested (and the records exist), it is possible to search through the history of the owners of your property all the way back to the earliest written land records. In doing so, you might be surprised what you'll learn about the history of your area. In some states, such as Georgia, land that was opened for settlement in the early 1800s was given away in lotteries.

Many areas in this country contained settlements of Native Americans as well. You may find references to reservations in early deeds. Looking at old maps of Indian trails or villages may help you discover the history of your area at that time.

Deeds before 1900 often measured property in chains, rods, and links. These units of measurement come from the old English system of measuring land called "metes and bounds." "Mete" is an old Anglo-Saxon word that means "to measure."

The surveyors actually used a chain 66 feet long when they surveyed land in this country in the 1800s. Around 1900, surveyors switched to feet and yards.

"The challenge comes in knowing where to look;
the reward is in rediscovering the past."
Researching the History of your House
Colorado Historical Society

Who Owned Your Land Before Your Home Appeared?

☞ *Good for all homes*

You may want to research the history of your land before your house was built. If you do, you often find one of three things:

1. The early landowners were people who were instrumental in the founding of your town — people whose names are now on a street sign, school, or library. (We like to think that towns were founded for altruistic reasons, but very often real estate speculators bought land along a river or a railroad, gave the area a name and tried to sell the real estate. If they

Your land may be located within the boundaries of an old farm in your area. The farmer's name may appear in local history books or old maps.

were successful and the town grew, the real estate investors were considered the "founding fathers.")

2. The landowners were a farming family. You might find the farm on an old landowner's map. Perhaps the old farmhouse still exists.

3. The landowners were from a wealthy family, perhaps in a nearby city. Land has always been a popular investment.

As you trace the history of your property back in time, you will probably find that you are researching a larger and larger area. For example, if your property description or "legal description" shows that you own a lot in a subdivision, researching back before the subdivision was created may show you that the subdivider bought the land from a farmer. So the property description will include a much larger area.

You may find that there are homestead records for your area at the Bureau of Land Management in your state (go to www.blm.gov/nhp/index.htm), or at your State Historic Preservation Office (see back of book for addresses).

Land-ownership maps that showed the location of farms in the 1800s and early 1900s are called "cadastral maps." Often, these maps were contained in county atlases. Look for these maps in libraries and historical societies.

Understanding How Land Was Surveyed

☞ *Good for all homes*

If you want to trace the history of your property back as far as possible, you will be delving into the history of land settlement in your area. Land that was surveyed or settled *before* the Revolutionary War was divided in a variety of ways depending on the history, geography, or the nationality of the people who first settled your area. Since this varies from area to area, look for specific information about this in your own state. This would be a good question to ask knowledgeable people at libraries and archives that you visit.

Land that was surveyed after the Revolutionary War (most of the Midwest and West) was done fairly systematically, using a system of lines running north-south and east-west six miles apart. These lines divided land into squares that measured six miles by six miles. Each of these six-mile squares was called a "township." I call these "surveyor's townships" so as not to be confused with named townships (York Township, Morris Township, etc.) in your area.

Each surveyor's township contained 36 square miles. Each of these square miles was called a "section." A section was one square mile and contained 640 acres. Each section of land had a section-township-range number to identify it.

The thirty-six sections in a surveyor's township were numbered in a specific (and rather interesting) way. Section one was always in the northeast corner of the surveyor's township. Section two was just to the west of section one. Sections three, four, five, and six followed to the west of each other. Section seven was immediately south of section six. Sections eight through 12 followed to the east. Section 13 was immediately south of section 12, and sections 14 though 18 followed as you headed west. This continued alternately heading east or west until you ended up in the southwest corner with section 36.

6	5	4	3	2	1
7	8	9	10	11	12
18	17	16	15	14	13
19	20	21	22	23	24
30	29	28	27	26	25
31	32	33	34	35	36

The preceding diagram indicates how the 36 sections in a surveyor's township were numbered.

The system of numbering sections in a township seems a bit odd until you learn that this system is called "boustrophedonic," which means "as the ox plows a field."

Land was often sold by the quarter section (one-quarter of a section) that contained 160 acres, and sometimes in pieces as small as one-quarter of a quarter section (40 acres).

Sometimes you encounter a long description such as "the east half of the southeast quarter of the southwest quarter of the southwest quarter." This is best understood when you decipher it (sketching it out helps) starting from the end.

1. Start by drawing a large one-mile square section, divide it into quarters, and outline the southwest quarter.

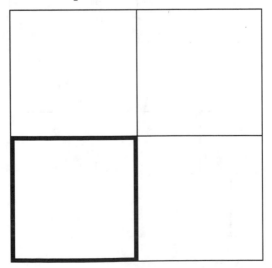

2. Divide the southwest quarter into quarters and outline the southwest quarter.

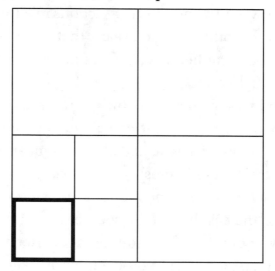

3. Divide that southwest quarter into quarters and outline the southeast quarter.

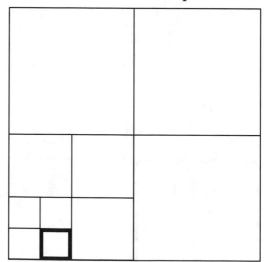

4. Divide that southeast quarter into east and west halves and shade the east half. You did it!

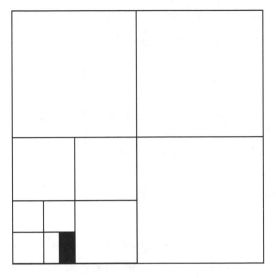

Land Measurement Trivia

Even though we don't use chains and rods to measure land anymore, these measurements have left their mark on the American landscape. Many streets have a 66-foot-wide right-of-way. (Sixty-six feet seems an odd width until you remember that there are 66 feet in a chain.)

The surveyors' 66-foot-long chain was invented in England several hundred years ago by Edmund Gunter. He figured out that if you measure a square or rectangular piece of land with 66-foot-long chains, multiply the length by the width, and move the decimal point one space to the left, the resulting figure will be the square acreage of that piece of land. This saved the surveyors' time back in the days before electronic calculators.

"N 18.5 Degrees 3 Chains 5 Links . . ."

☛ *Good for all homes*

Even if you live in an area of the country where land is divided into nice square pieces called "sections," people don't always sell land in squares or rectangles. This often happens when land borders a lake, stream, or road with an irregular shape. Land that has not been subdivided (such as farmland) is sometimes described this way when the property has an irregular shape.

Usually these land descriptions in deeds start off with something like, "By commencing at a stake at the south side of a nine-inch-diameter red oak stump in the quarter sectionline . . ." Don't worry about the trees. They were used by the surveyor to help him find his stakes and are usually not crucial to the land description. (The tree descriptions *can* give you an idea of what kind of trees existed on your land when the surveyor walked the area, however.) If the surveyor used wooden stakes, the stakes won't be there either.

Each phrase that contains a compass reading and a measurement length is a surveyor's "call." (See the section "Untangling Land Measurements" on page 191 to help you sort out the meanings of chains, rods, and links.)

If you're lucky, a deed description will contain only a few calls and they will all be either north, south, east, or west. That is fairly easy to figure out by sketching out the shape described. If some of the calls include directions such as "NE 24 degrees" or "SW 110 degrees," the next section will help you.

"Getting to know the history of your house can be a fun and fascinating process."

HOUSE HISTORIC RESEARCH GUIDE

NANCY COMPAU, SPOKANE PUBLIC LIBRARY

"North 15 Degrees East 13 Chains, East 8 Chains. . ."

☞ *Good for all homes*

Some pieces of property are very irregular and are described on the deed by a long list of surveyor's calls. Each call consists of a direction and a distance. (The title of this section is composed of two calls.) If the description on a deed contains phrases such as the ones in the title above, you'll probably want to get a Land Measure Compass no. A-26 (ordering information on page 190) and sketch out the shape of the land. You can make do with a protractor, but it's somewhat awkward.

Here's how to figure it out. The 360 degrees of a circle are divided by two lines into four pie-shaped pieces; one line connects north and south, one connects east and west. Each piece contains 90 degrees.

It helps to create a diagram as you read the surveyor's calls. Using graph paper will help you keep track of the four cardinal directions.

Here's an example of a surveyor's description: "Commencing at a stake in the center of the section, thence north 15 degrees east 13 chains, thence east 8 chains, thence south 15 degrees west 13 chains, thence west 8 chains to the point of beginning."

This can be figured out in four steps:

1. "Commencing at a stake in the center of the section, thence north 15 degrees east 13 chains"

Make a dark mark to use as your beginning point. Place your protractor or land compass so that this point (often called the "point of beginning" or "POB" in deeds) is in the center and even with the 0 degree mark. North is above your starting point, and east is directly right of your starting point. Starting at north, measure 15 degrees to the right (east). This will give you the angle for "north 15 degrees east." Make a light pencil mark on the outside of your land measure compass or protractor.

Use a ruler to measure 13 chains at this angle start-ing from your point of beginning. Decide what scale you are going to use to relate chains and links to the inches or centimeters on your ruler. (For small pieces of property, you might want to set 1 chain = 1/4 inch on your ruler.) Make a second dark mark at the 13 chains point.

Step 1. Thence north 15° east 13 chains

P.O.B.

2. "thence east 8 chains"

Place your land measure compass or protractor so that your second mark is in the center and even with the 0 degree mark. Since this direction is due east, measure 8 chains directly to the right and make a third dark mark.

Step 2. Thence east 8 chains

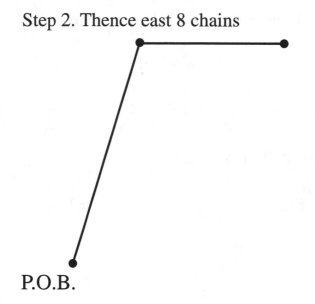

P.O.B.

3. "thence south 15 degrees west 13 chains"

Place your land measure compass or protractor so that your third mark is in the center. South is directly below your mark, and west is directly to the left. Starting from south, measure 15 degrees to the left (west), and make a light mark. This will give you the angle for "south 15 degrees west." Use a ruler to measure 13 chains at this angle starting from your third mark. Make a fourth dark mark.

Step 3. Thence south 15° west 13 chains

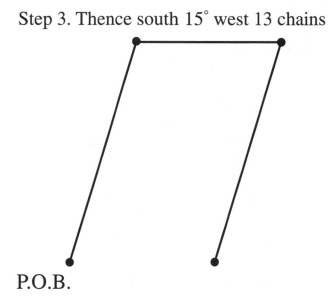

P.O.B.

4. "thence west 8 chains to the point of beginning."

Place your land measure compass or protractor so that your fourth mark is in the center. West is directly left, so use a ruler to measure 8 chains due west. If you measured correctly (and if the surveyor did his job correctly), you should end up where you began. If you suspect there's an error in the description, look for the same land description on a previous or subsequent deed. Compare the calls and figure out the error. Some surveyors wrote their "Ns" and "Ws" so similarly that it's hard to tell them apart.

Step 4. Thence west 8 chains to the point of beginning

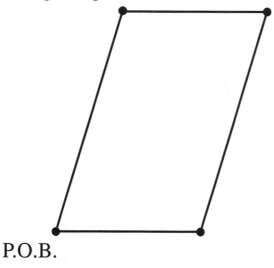

P.O.B.

Surveyors also varied the way that they described angles. Sometimes they wrote "NE 24 degrees," other times they wrote "N 24 degrees E." Either way it's the same. Sometimes they wrote "NE 110 degrees" – that's the same as "SE 70 degrees."

Note: You can order the Land Measure Compass no. A-26 by contacting Alpine Import Craft Supplies at 800-654-6114 or info@alpineimport.com.

Untangling Land Measurements

☛ *Good for all homes*

If you're delving into deeds that date from the 1800s, you may find land measured in units such as those below. You'll probably want to convert these to feet and inches.

Linear Measurements:
1 link = 7.92 inches
1 rod (pole) = 16.5 feet
1 chain = 66 feet
80 chains = 1 mile
320 rods = 1 mile
8,000 links = 1 mile

Square Measurements:
640 acres = 1 square mile
1 section = 1 square mile
36 square miles = 1 township
6,400 square chains = 640 acres

How They Fit Together:
1 rod = 25 links
1 chain = 4 rods
1 chain = 100 links
1 mile = 320 rods
1 acre = 10 square chains

If you've ever wondered why a mile is 5,280 feet long, or why an acre is *about* 208 feet square, it's because feet and inches are not part of the traditional system of measuring land.

In some parts of the country, early deeds may contain land measurements using other types of units such as "varas," "arpents," etc. Ask about these at historical societies or libraries in your area.

Landownership Maps Contain Landowners' Names

☞ *Good for rural and suburban homes*

If you live on the outskirts of town, or in an old farm house, landownership maps can be useful. You might learn which farmer owned your land before it was developed.

The technical term for land ownership maps is "cadastral maps." Many people simply call them "farm ownership maps."

Cadastral maps are often found in county atlases. These atlases were published in the 1800s and early 1900s and contained much more information than road maps. They often contained the history of the county, townships and towns, as well as sketches of homes, their owners and biographies. People usually paid for a biographical listing in these atlases, and of course, the county atlas was prominently displayed in the front parlor, right next to the family bible.

These maps are particularly useful if you live in a county that uses the grantor/grantee index to deeds. If a deed was not recorded, you can use the farm ownership maps to figure out the farm owner's name. Then, search for that name going forward in the grantor books or backward in the grantee books.

Agricultural Censuses Yield Farm Information

☛ *Good for rural homes built 1850–1880*

Do you live in an old farmhouse? Look for copies of the "Nonpopulation Census Schedules" for your state. Ask at libraries, historical societies, or the nearest branch of the National Archives and Records Administration. Sometimes these are called the "farm censuses" or the "agricultural censuses," which are more descriptive terms. This type of census won't tell you much about your house, but it will provide very detailed information about how many acres of wheat, corn, or oats were grown on the farm; how many head of cattle, dairy cows, sheep, horses, oxen, were raised, etc.

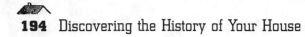

Farm or agricultural censuses will provide insight into how the land was used on the farm that surrounded your old farmhouse in the late 1800s.

Making Your Own History

Put Your Research Finds in Order

☛ *Good for all homes*

As you begin to accumulate information about the history of your house throughout the research process, arrange the information in chronological order. Very often, the events concerning the past of your house make more sense if viewed in the order in which they occurred.

You can do this on a computer with a software program that sorts numbers. Even a word-processing program can be used to sort if you start each paragraph with a date. If you're dealing with papers, place them in chronological order as well.

Save Your Research and Memorabilia

☛ *Good for all homes*

Once you begin doing research, collecting information, or recording changes and events that have taken place in your home, you'll want to store these items so that future owners of your home will not have to sift through crumbling, yellowing pieces of paper. Look for paper and storage boxes that have the words "archival," "acid-free," "lignin-free," or "photo-safe" on the label. These items can be found in photo stores, stationary stores, craft stores, and scrapbook shops.

Original documents and newspaper clippings, etc., should be photocopied onto archival-quality paper. You can bring archival-quality paper with you to a copy shop and substitute it for their standard paper.

Before you store any photos, label the back of each one and identify the subject or subjects in the photo, where the photo was taken, and the date of the photo. To label the backs of photos, buy a "woodless" graphite pencil from an art supply store. This kind of pencil is simply a cylinder of soft graphite and will not harm the photos. Neither will it fade over time as ink does.

Videotapes and audiotapes will degrade in a matter of years. Do not rely on these to store archival information. Also consider how difficult it will be to access these tapes if the technology changes. Suppose you had stored important information on an eight-track cassette tape or a Betamax videotape.

Black and white photos will last for many years, and are preferred by museums for archival photography. Color snapshots and slides fade after a while. Polaroid photos fade even faster. Storing images on CDs is not recommended because of the problems of finding equipment 20 or 50 years from now that will be compatible with today's electronic media.

Store each photo in a separate plastic sleeve, or use special corner holders that affix photos to scrapbook pages. Make sure that both the pages and the corner holders are marked "archival." Plastic sleeves should also be archival quality. Polyester, Mylar, polyethylene, and polypropylene are all safe materials. Avoid anything made of PVC (polyvinyl chloride) or vinyl.

Use archival adhesive materials only. Do not use cellophane tape (it yellows, dries, and stains), or metal paper clips or staples (they rust and stain).

Store items in an archival box. The best place to store a box or album is in a closet or drawer. This will protect it from light. Avoid storing your box or album in an attic or basement. These areas are prone to dampness or extreme heat.

If local stores don't stock the kind of storage containers that you need, ask if you can order one. If you're still not having any luck, contact local museums and ask if they know where to obtain archival storage boxes. You can also use the Internet to locate companies that make archival materials and containers.

———•———

"No matter how many wonderful discoveries you make, the information you uncover will only be useful to you and others if you are careful to record what you find out."
How to Research the History of Your Home in New Castle County, Delaware
Susan Brizzolara and Valerie Cesna

Start Your Own Photo Archive

☞ *Good for all homes*

Take photos of significant events such as snowstorms or floods, birthday and graduation parties, and weddings that occur in your home, and store the photos in an *archival* or *photo-safe* box or album. Remember to label the back of the photos with a soft graphite woodless pencil (available at art supply stores) with dates, descriptions, and names of people. Take before and after photos of changes that you make to the house. If you find anything interesting inside the walls when doing renovations or repairs, photograph this as well.

Give Something Back to Your Local Historical Society

☞ *Good for all homes*

When you've finished researching your house, or as you find interesting information about it, considering donating a copy of your findings to your local historical society. You've probably already spent time doing research there, and it would be nice to give something back to them. It would also act as extra insurance in case you misplace your copy of that item. Your research efforts may help or inspire other vintage homeowners in their research. Remember that although you may leave your research in the home when you sell it, there's no guarantee that future owners of your home will value (and save) all of your hard work.

Other Sources of Information

State Historic Preservation Offices

Following is a state-by-state guide to state historic preservation offices and useful materials I've found. You can expand your search by asking for booklets about house history research at local libraries, historical societies, and historic or landmark commissions. Don't forget to check the Internet.

Alabama

Dr. Lee H. Warner
State Historic Preservation Officer & Executive Director
Alabama Historical Commission
468 South Perry St.
Montgomery, AL 36130-0900
Phone: 334-242-3184
A Guide to Researching Old Buildings in Alabama. National Register Division, Alabama Historical Commission.

McCorquodale Burkhardt, Ann. *House Detective: Guide to Researching Birmingham Buildings.* Birmingham Historical Society, One Sloss Quarters, Birmingham, 35222, telephone 205-251-1880, www.bhistorical.org

Alaska

Ms. Judith Bittner
State Historic Preservation Officer
Division of Natural Resources
Division of Parks & Outdoor Rec.
550 W. 7th Ave., Ste. 1310
Anchorage, AK 99510-3565
Phone: 907-269-8721
E-mail: judyb@dnr.state.ak.us

Arizona
Mr. James W. Garrison
State Historic Preservation Officer
Office of Historic Preservation
Arizona State Parks
1300 West Washington
Phoenix, AZ 85007
Phone: 602-542-4174
E-mail: jgarrison@pr.state.az.us

Arkansas
Ms. Cathie Matthews
State Historic Preservation Officer
Dept. of Arkansas Heritage
323 Center Street, Ste. 1500
Little Rock, AR 72201
Phone: 501-324-9162
E-mail: cathie@arkansasheritage.org

California
Dr. W. Knox Mellon
State Historic Preservation Officer
Office of Historic Preservation
Dept. of Parks and Rec.
P.O. Box 942896
Sacramento, CA 94296-0001
Phone: 916-653-6624
E-mail: dabey@ohp.parks.ca.gov

Powell, John Edward and Enns-Rempel, Kevin. *Historic Residence Research Resources: A Guide for the Layperson to Sources of Building Data in Fresno.* www.fresno.edu/preserve/resource.htm.

Colorado
Ms. Georgianna Contiguglia
State Historic Preservation Officer
Colorado History Museum
1300 Broadway
Denver, CO 80203-2137
Phone: 303-866-3355
E-mail: www.coloradohistory-oahp.org
Researching the History of Your House. Colorado Historical Society, 1999.

Connecticut
Mr. John W. Shannahan
State Historic Preservation Officer and Director
Connecticut Historical Commission
59 South Prospect St.
Hartford, CT 06106
Phone: 860-566-3005
E-mail: cthist@neca.com

Delaware
Mr. Daniel Griffith
State Historic Preservation Officer
Division of History and Cultural Affairs

Hall of Records
121 Duke of York St.
Dover, DE 19901
Phone: 302-739-5313
E-mail: dgriffith@state.de.us
Cesna, Valerie and Brizolara, Susan. *How to Research the History of Your Home in New Castle County, Delaware.* New Castle County Department of Planning, 1996.

District of Columbia
Mr. Gregory McCarthy
State Historic Preservation Officer
Office of Policy & Program Evaluation
801 N. Capitol St., Suite 3000
Washington, D.C. 20002
Phone: 202-442-8818
E-mail: gregory.mccarthy@dc.gov

Florida
Dr. Janet Snyder Matthews
State Historic Preservation Officer
Div. of Historical Resources
R.A. Gray Bldg.
500 S. Bronough St.
Tallahassee, FL 32399-0250
Phone: 850-245-6300
E-mail: jmatthews@mail.dos.state.fl

Georgia

Mr. Lonice C. Barrett
State Historic Preservation Officer
Dept. of Natural Resources
156 Trinity Ave., SW, Ste. 101
Atlanta, GA 30303
Phone: 404-656-3500
E-mail: lonice_barrett@mail.dnr.state.ga.us
Thomas, Jr., Ken H. *Documenting a Historic Structure in Atlanta.* Historic Preservation Division, Georgia Department of Natural Resources.

Hawaii

Mr. Gilbert Coloma-Agaran
State Historic Preservation Officer
Dept. of Land and Natural Resources
601 Kamokila Blvd., Rm. 555
Kapolei, HI 96707
Phone: 808-587-0401
E-mail: dlnr@exec.state.hi.us

Idaho

Mr. Steve Guerber
State Historic Preservation Officer
State Historic Preservation Office
210 Main St.
Boise, ID 83702-7264
Phone: 208-334-3890
E-mail: kreid@ishs.state.id.us

Attebery, Jennifer Eastman and Ford, Guila. *A Guide to Documenting the History of a Building.* Reference Series 741. Idaho State Historical Society, 1983.

Illinois

Mr. William L. Wheeler

State Historic Preservation Officer

Illinois Historic Preservation Agency

Preservation Services Division

1 Old State Capitol Plaza

Springfield, IL 62701

Phone: 217-785-9045

E-mail: historicpreservation@yahoo.com

Koos, Greg. *Researching Your Illinois House.* Springfield, Illinois: Illinois Historic Preservation Agency, 1986.

Indiana

Mr. Larry D. Macklin

State Historic Preservation Officer

Department of Natural Resources

402 W. Washington St., Rm. W274

Indianapolis, IN 46204

Phone: 317-232-4020

E-mail: dhpa@dnr.state.in.us

Handbook for Historical Building Research. Indianapolis Historic Preservation Commission.

Historic House Research Handbook: Focus on Local History, Number 1. Historic Landmarks Foundation of Indiana, Indiana Historical Bureau.

This Old House. Indianapolis-Marion County Public Library web site at www.imcpl.org/ss_hshis.htm

Iowa

Ms. Anita Walker
Actg. State Historic Preservation Officer
State Historical Society of Iowa
600 E. Locust St.
Des Moines, IA 50319-0290
Phone: 515-281-8837
E-mail: anitawalker@dca.state.ia.us

Kansas

Dr. Ramon S. Powers
State Historic Preservation Officer
Kansas State Historical Society
Cultural Resources Div.
6425 SW 6th Ave.
Topeka, KS 66615-1099
Phone: 785-272-8681
E-mail: histsoc@acc.wuacc.edu

Guide to Research Resources in the Library and Archives Division of the Kansas State Historical Society and *Researching Old Buildings*, Kansas State Historical Society.

Kentucky
Mr. David Morgan
State Historic Preservation Officer
Kentucky Heritage Council
300 Washington St.
Frankfort, KY 40601
Phone: 502-564-7005
E-mail: dmorgan@mail.stateky.us

Louisiana
Mrs. Laurel Wyckoff
State Historic Preservation Officer
Office of Cultural Dev.
P.O. Box 44247
Baton Rouge, LA 70804
Phone: 225-342-8160
E-mail: hp@crt.state.la.us
Everard, Wayne M. *How to Research the History of Your House (or Other Building) in New Orleans.* New Orleans: Friends of New Orleans Public Library, 1986. nutrias.org/guides/house/title.htm

Maine
Mr. Earle Shettleworth, Jr.
State Historic Preservation Officer
Maine Historic Preservation Commission
55 Capitol St., Station 65
Augusta, ME 04333-0065
Phone: 207-287-2132
E-mail: earl.shettleworth@state.me.us

Maryland
Mr. J. Rodney Little
State Historic Preservation Officer
Dept. of Housing and Community Development
Peoples Resource Ctr.
100 Community Place, 3rd Floor
Crownsville, MD 21032-2023
Phone: 410-514-7600
E-mail: mdshpo@ari.net

Massachusetts
Ms. Elsa Fitzgerald
Actg. Executive Director
Massachusetts Historical Commission
Massachusetts Archives Facility
220 Morrissey Blvd.
Boston, MA 02125
Phone: 617-727-8470
E-mail: judy.mcdonough@sec.state.ma.us

Michigan
Mr. Brian Conway
State Historic Preservation Officer
Bureau of Michigan History
717 W. Allegan
Lansing, MI 489180001
Phone: 517-373-0511
E-mail: conwaybd@sosmail.state.mi.us

Minnesota
Dr. Nina M. Archabal
State Historic Preservation
Minnesota Historical Society
State Historic Preservation Office
345 Kellogg Blvd. West
St. Paul, MN 55102
Phone: 612-296-2747
E-mail: mnshpo@mnhs.org

Mississippi
Mr. Elbert Hilliard
State Historic Preservation Officer
Mississippi Dept. Archives and History
P.O. Box 571
Jackson, MS 39205
Phone: 601-359-6850
E-mail: msshpo@mdah.ms.us

Missouri
Mr. Steven Mahfood
State Historic Preservation Officer
State Dept. of Natural Resources
P.O. Box 176
Jefferson City, MO 65102
Phone: 573-751-4732
E-mail: mmiles@mail.more.net

Montana

D. Mark F. Baumler
State Historic Preservation Officer
Montana Historical Society
1410 8th Avenue
P.O. Box 201202
Helena, MT 59620-1202
Phone: 406-444-7717
E-mail: mbaumler@state.mt.us
National Register of Historic Places Workbook, State Historic Preservation Office, Montana Historical Society.

Nebraska

Mr. Lawrence J. Sommer
State Historic Preservation Officer
Nebraska State Historical Society
1500 R. St.
P.O. Box 82554
Lincoln, NE 68501
Phone: 402-471-4746
E-mail: nshs@nebraskahistory.org

Nevada

Mr. Ronald M. James
State Historic Preservation Officer
Dept. of Museums, Library and Arts
100 N. Stewart St., Capitol Complex
Carson City, NV 89701-4285

E-mail: rmjames@clan.lib.nv.us
How to Prepare Nominations to the National Register
of Historic Places: A Guide for Nevada Property Owners.
Nevada State Historic Preservation Office, 1999.

New Hampshire
Ms. Nancy C. Dutton
State Historic Preservation Officer
Division of Historical Resources
P.O. Box 2043
Concord, NH 03302-2043
Phone: 603-271-6435
E-mail: ndutton@nhdhr.state.nh.us

New Jersey
Nr. Robert C. Shinn, Jr.
State Historic Preservation Officer
NJ Dept. Parks & Forestry
P.O. Box 304
Trenton, NJ 08625-0404
Phone: 609-292-2885
E-mail: njhpo@dep.state.nj.us

New Mexico
Mr. Elmo Baca
State Historic Preservation Officer
Office of Cultural Affairs
Villa Rivera Bldg., 3rd Fl.
228 E. Palace Ave.

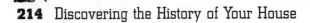

Sante Fe, NM 87503
Phone: 505-827-6320
E-mail: ebaca@lvr.state.nm.us
McHugh, Floyd. *Sources & Searches: Documenting Historic Buildings in New Mexico.* New Mexico Historic Preservation Division, 1985.

New York
Mrs. Bernadette Castro
State Historic Preservation Officer
Office of Parks, Recreation and Historic Pres.
Empire State Plaza
Agency Bldg 1, 20th Fl.
Albany, NY 12238
Phone: 518-474-0443
E-mail: j.aldrich@oprhp.state.ny.us

North Carolina
Dr. Jeffrey J. Crow
State Historic Preservation Officer
Dept. of Cultural Resources
Division of Archives and History
4617 Mail Service Ct.
Raleigh, NC 27699-4617
Phone: 919-733-7305
E-mail: arcy.mam@ncdcr.state.nc.us
How to Research the History of Real Estate. Charlotte-Mecklenburg Historic Landmarks Commission, www.cmhpf.org/resources/researching.html

North Dakota

Mr. Merl E. Paaverud
Interim Superintendent
State Historical Society of North Dakota
ND Heritage Ctr.
612 E. Boulevard Ave.
Bismarck, ND 58505-0830
Phone: 701-328-2666
E-mail: swegner@state.nd.us

Ohio

Dr. Amos J. Loveday, Jr.
State Historic Preservation Officer
Ohio Historic Preservation Office
Ohio Historical Society
567 E. Hudson St.
Columbus, OH 43211-1030
Phone: 614-298-2000
E-mail: ajloveday@aol.com
Dating a Structure. Greene County Public Library
at www.gcpl.lib.oh.us/services/ger/hist_res/dating.html

Oklahoma

Dr. Bob L. Blackburn
State Historic Preservation Officer
Oklahoma Historical Society
Wiley Post Historical Bldg.
2100 N. Lincoln Blvd.
Oklahoma City, OK 73105

Phone: 405-521-2491

E-mail: jgabbert@ok-history.mus.ok.us

Oregon

Mr. Mike Carrier

State Historic Preservation Officer

Oregon Parks and Recreation Dept.

1115 Commercial St. NE

Salem, OR 97310-1002

Phone: 503-378-4168

E-mail: shpop.info@state.or.us

Pennsylvania

Dr. Brent D. Glass

State Historic Preservation Officer

Pennsylvania Historical and Museum Com.

Commonwealth Keystone Bldg.

400 North St.

Harrisburg, PA 17120-0093

Phone: 717-787-2891

E-mail: bglass@state.pa.us

Munger, Donna Bingham. *Pennsylvania Land Records: A History and Guide for Research.* Pennsylvania Historical and Museum Commission, 1991.

Rhode Island

Mr. Frederick C. Williamson

State Historic Preservation Officer

Historic Preservation and Heritage Comm.

Old State House

150 Benefit St.

Providence, RI 02903

Phone: 401-222-2678

E-mail: esanderson@rihpc.state.ri.us

Lamar, Christine, ed. *Uncovering the History of Your House*. Providence, Rhode Island: Rhode Island Historical Society, 1987.

South Carolina

Dr. Rodger E. Stroup

State Historic Preservation Officer

Dept. of Archives and History

8301 Parkland Rd.

Columbia, SC 29223-4905

Phone: 803-896-6185

E-mail: edmonds@scdah.state.sc.us

South Dakota

Mr. Jay D. Vogt

State Historic Preservation Officer

South Dakota State Historical Society

900 Governors Drive

Pierre, SD 57501-2217

Phone: 605-773-3458

E-mail: jay.vogt@state.sd.us

Tennessee
Mr. Milton H. Hamilton, Jr.
State Historic Preservation Officer
Dept. of Environment and Conservation
2941 Lebanon Rd.
Nashville, TN 37243-0442
Phone: 615-532-0109
E-mail: susanpierce@wvculture.org

Texas
Mr. Lawrence Oaks
State Historic Preservation Officer
Texas Historical Commission
P.O. Box 12276
Capitol Station
Austin, TX 78711-2276
Phone 512-463-6100
E-mail: l.oaks@thc.state.tx.us
Texas Preservation Guidelines – Remembering Texas: Guidelines for Historical Research. Texas Historical Commission, 1998.

Utah
Mr. Max J. Evans
State Historic Preservation Office
Utah State Historical Society
300 Rio Grande
Salt Lake City, UT 84101
Phone: 801-533-3551

E-mail: ushs@history.state.ut.us

Intensive Level Survey: Standard Operating Procedures.
Utah Office of Preservation, 1993.

Vermont
Ms. Emily Wadhams
State Historic Preservation Officer
Agency of Commerce & Community Dev.
VT Division for Hist. Preservation
National Life Bldg., Drawer 20
Montpelier, VT 05620-0501
Phone: 802-828-3056
E-mail: ewadhams@gate.dce.state.vt.us

Virginia
Ms. Kathleen S. Kilpatrick
State Historic Preservation Officer
Dept. of Historic Resources
2801 Kensington Ave.
Richmond, VA 23221
Phone: 804-367-2323
E-mail: kkilpatrick@dhr.state.va.us

Washington
Dr. Allyson Brooks
State Historic Preservation Officer
Office of Archeology & Historic Preservation
1063 S. Capitol Way, Ste. 106
P.O. Box 48343

Olympia, WA 98504-8343
Phone: 360-585-3066
E-mail: allysonb@cted.wa.gov
Compau, Nancy. *House Historic Research Guide.*
City of Spokane, 1999, www.historicspokane.org/
guide34.htm

West Virginia

Ms. Nancy Herholdt
State Historic Preservation Officer
Division of Culture and History
1900 Kanawha Blvd. East
Charleston, WV 25305
Phone: 304-558-0220
E-mail: susan.pierce@wvculture.org

Wisconsin

Dr. George L. Vogt
State Historic Preservation Officer
Wisconsin State Historical Society
816 State St.
Madison, WI 53706-1482
Phone: 608-264-6500
E-mail: glvogt@mail.shsw.wisc.edu
Tracing the History of Your House. McIntyre
Library, University of Wisconsin, Eau Claire at
www.uwec.edu/library/guides/househist.html

Researching Old Buildings. State Historical Society
of Wisconsin, 1996.

Wyoming
Mr. Richard Curritt
State Historic Preservation Officer
Wyoming State Historic Preservation Office
Dept. of State Parks & Cultural Resources
2301 Central Ave., 3rd Fl.
Cheyenne, WY 82002
Phone: 307-777-7697
E-mail: rcurri@stte.wy.us

Regional Depository Libraries

These libraries hold an assortment of files and records that are too bulky or numerous to be stored in local facilities. Contact them and ask for a list of their holdings. Some may allow you to access their catalog via the Internet. Also ask if there are regional depositories in your state that are closer to you. Items stored at regional depository libraries might include Sanborn Fire Insurance Maps, other old maps, tax assessors' records, probate records, estate inventory records, court case files, records of births, deaths, and marriages, etc.

Alabama
Regional Depository Library
Auburn University at Montgomery
PO Box 244023
Library, Government Documents

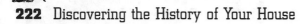

Montgomery, AL 36124-4023
334-244-3200

Regional Depository Library
University of Alabama Libraries
PO Box 870266
Tuscaloosa, AL 35487-0266
205-348-7561

Alaska
Regional Depository Library
Washington State Library
MS AJ-11
Olympia, WA 98504
206-753-4035

Arizona
Regional Depository Library
Department of Library
Archives and Public Records
State Capitol, Rm. 200
1700 W. Washington
Phoenix, AZ 85007
602-542-4417

Arkansas
Regional Depository Library
Arkansas State Library
Documents Service Section

1 Capitol Mall
Little Rock, AR 72201
501-682-1527

California
Regional Depository Library
California State Library
Government Publications Section
PO Box 942837
Sacramento, CA 94237-0001
916-654-0183

Colorado
Regional Depository Library
University of Colorado at Boulder
Government Publications Library
Campus Box 184
Boulder, CO 80309-0184
303-492-7511

Regional Depository Library
Denver Public Library
Government Publications Department
1000 14th Ave. Pkwy.
Denver, CO 80204-2749
303-640-6200

Connecticut
Regional Depository Library

Connecticut State Library
231 Capitol Ave.
Hartford, CT 06106
860-566-4777

Delaware
Regional Depository Library
University of Maryland
McKeldin Library
Documents – Map Room
College Park, MD 20742-4345
301-405-2038

District of Columbia
Regional Depository Library
District of Columbia
University of Maryland
McKeldin Library
Documents – Map Room
College Park, MD 20742-4345
301-405-2038

Florida
Regional Depository Library
University of Florida Libraries
Documents Department
PO Box 117001
Library West
Gainesville, FL 32611
352-392-0342

Georgia
Regional Depository Library
University of Georgia Libraries
Government Documents Department
Athens, GA 30602
706-542-0621

Hawaii
Regional Depository Library
University of Hawaii
Hamilton Library
Government Documents Collection
2550 The Mall
Honolulu, HI 96822-2550
808-956-7203

Idaho
Regional Depository Library
University of Idaho Libraries
Documents Section
Moscow, ID 83844-2350
208-885-6534

Illinois
Regional Depository Library
Illinois State Library
Federal Documents
300 S. 2nd St.
Springfield, IL 62701-1976
217-782-7596

Indiana
Regional Depository Library
Indiana State Library
Serials and Documents
140 N. Senate Ave.
Indianapolis, IN 46204
317-232-3675

Iowa
Regional Depository Library
University of Iowa Libraries
Government Publications Department
Iowa City, IA 52242-1420
319-335-5867

Kansas
Regional Depository Library
University of Kansas
Spencer Research Library
Government Documents & Maps
Lawrence, KS 66045-2800
913-864-3456

Kentucky
Regional Depository Library
University of Kentucky Libraries
Government Publications – Maps
Lexington, KY 40506-0456
606-257-0500

Louisiana

Regional Depository Library
Louisiana State University
Middletown Library
Government Documents Department
Baton Rouge, LA 70803-3300
504-388-2217

Regional Depository Library
Louisiana Technical University
Prescott Memorial Library
PO Box 10408
Documents Department
Ruston, LA 71272-0046
318-257-3555

Maine

Regional Depository Library
University of Maine
Raymond Fogler Library
Government Documents
Orono, ME 04469-5729
207-581-1661
www.umaine.edu-Index-libcom.htm

Maryland

Regional Depository Library
University of Maryland
McKeldin Library

Documents – Map Room
College Park, MD 20742-4345
301-405-9128

Massachusetts
Regional Depository Library
Boston Public Library
Government Documents
666 Boylston St.
Boston, MA 02117-0286
617-536-5400

Michigan
Regional Depository Library
Detroit Public Library
5201 Woodward Ave.
Detroit, MI 48202-4007
313-833-1000

Regional Depository Library
Library of Michigan
Government Documents Service
717 W. Allegan St.
PO Box 30007
Lansing, MI 48909
517-373-1580

Minnesota
Regional Depository Library

University of Minnesota
409 Wilson Library
Government Publications Library
309 S. 19th St.
Minneapolis, MN 55455-0414
612-624-4520

Mississippi
Regional Depository Library
University of Mississippi
Williams Library
Documents Department
University, MS 38677
601-232-6824

Missouri
Regional Depository Library
University of Missouri at Columbia
Ellis Library
Government Documents
Columbia, MO 65201-5149
573-882-4701

Montana
Regional Depository Library
University of Montana
Maurene and Mike Mansfield Library
Documents Department
Missoula, MT 59812
406-243-6860

Nebraska
Regional Depository Library
University of Nebraska at Lincoln
Love Library
PO Box 880410
Federal Documents Department
Lincoln, NE 68588-0410
402-472-2526

Nevada
Regional Depository Library
University of Nevada Library
Government Publications Department
Reno, NV 89557-0044
702-784-6500

New Hampshire
Regional Depository Library
University of Maine
Raymond Fogler Library
Government Documents
Orono, ME 04469-5729
207-581-1681
www.umaine.edu-Index-libcom.htm

New Jersey
Regional Depository Library
Newark Public Library
US Documents Division

PO Box 630
5 Washington St.
Newark, NJ 07101
973-733-7800

New Mexico
Regional Depository Library
University of New Mexico
General Library
Government Publications & Maps Department
Alburquerque, NM 87131
505-277-4241

Regional Depository Library
New Mexico State Library
Documents Department
325 Don Gaspar Ave.
Santa Fe, NM 87503
505-827-3800

New York
Regional Depository Library
New York State Library
Legislative and Governmental Service
Cultural Education Center
Empire State Plaza
Albany, NY 12230
518-474-5930

North Carolina
Regional Depository Library
University of North Carolina at Chapel Hill
Davis Library
CB #3912 BA-SS
Department – Documents
Chapel Hill, NC 27514-8890
919-962-1301

North Dakota
Regional Depository Library
North Dakota State University Library
Documents Office
PO Box 5599
Fargo, ND 58105
701-231-8886

Regional Depository Library
University of North Dakota
Chester Fritz Library
PO Box 9000
Documents Department
Grand Forks, ND 58202-9000
701-777-4631

Ohio
Regional Depository Library
State Library of Ohio
Documents Section

65 S. Front St.
Columbus, OH 43215-4163
614-644-7061

Oklahoma
Regional Depository Library
Oklahoma Department of Libraries
Government Documents Division
200 N.E. 18th St.
Oklahoma City, OK 73105-3298
405-521-2502

Regional Depository Library
Oklahoma State University Library
Documents Department
Stillwater, OK 74708-1071
405-744-9729

Oregon
Regional Depository Library
Portland State University
Millar Library
PO Box 1151
Portland, OR 97207-1151
503-725-4617

Pennsylvania
Regional Depository Library
State Library of Pennsylvania

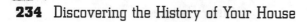

Government Publications
PO Box 1601
Harrisburg, PA 17105-1601
717-787-4440

Rhode Island
Regional Depository Library
Connecticut State Library
231 Capitol Ave.
Hartford, CT 06106
203-566-4971

South Carolina
Regional Depository Library
Clemson University
Cooper Library
Documents Department
Clemson, SC 29634-3001
864-656-3026

Regional Depository Library
University of South Carolina
Thomas Cooper Library
Documents – Microform Department
Sumter and Green Sts.
Columbia, SC 29208-0103
803-777-3142

South Dakota
Regional Depository Library
University of South Dakota
I.D. Weeks Library
414 E. Clark St.
Vermillion, SD 57069
605-677-5371

Tennessee
Regional Depository Library
Memphis State University Library
Government Documents Department
Memphis, TN 38152
901-678-2206

Texas
Regional Depository Library
Texas State Library
Documents Department
PO Box 12927
Capitol Station
Austin, TX 78711
512-463-5432

Regional Depository Library
Texas Technical University Library
Documents Department
Lubbock, TX 79409-0002
806-742-2261

Utah
Regional Depository Library
Utah State University
Merrill Library
UMC-30
Government Documents Department
Logan, UT 84322-3000
435-797-2631

Vermont
Regional Depository Library
University of Maine
Raymond Fogler Library
Government Documents
Orono, ME 04469-5729
207-581-1681
www.umaine.edu-Index-libcom.htm

Virginia
Regional Depository Library
University of Virginia
Alderman Library
Government Documents Department
Charlottesville, VA 22903-2498
804-924-3026

Washington
Regional Depository Library
Washington State Library

MS AJ-11
PO Box 42460
Olympia, WA 98504-2460
360-753-5590

West Virginia
Regional Depository Library
West Virginia University Library
Government Documents Section
Morgantown, WV 26506-6069
304-293-4040

Wisconsin
Regional Depository Library
State Historical Society of Wisconsin Library
Government Publications Section
816 State St.
Madison, WI 53706
608-264-6534

Regional Depository Library
Milwaukee Public Library
Documents Department
814 W. Wisconsin Ave.
Milwaukee, WI 53233-2385
414-286-3000

Wyoming
Regional Depository Library
Utah State University
Merrill Library
UMC-30
Government Documents Department
Logan, UT 84322-3000
435-797-2631

State Libraries

Most states have state libraries that may hold records useful to house history hunters. Ask if you can look at the catalog on the Internet. State libraries may have microfilm copies of old newspapers, vintage phone books, files on prominent citizens, old maps, etc.

Alabama
Alabama Department of Archives and History
624 Washington Ave.
Montgomery, AL 36139-0100
Phone: 334-242-4435
Website: www.apls.state.al.us

Alaska
Alaska State Library
P.O. Box 110571
Juneau, AK 99811

Phone: 907-465-2920
Website: www.library.state.ak.us/

Arizona
Arizona State Library
Archives and Public Services
State Capitol, Suite 342
1700 W. Washington
Phoenix, AZ 85007
Phone: 602-542-4035
Fax: 602-542-4972
Website: www.dlapr.lib.az.us/

Arkansas
Arkansas State Library
One Capitol Mall
Little Rock, AR 72201
Phone: 501-682-2053
Fax: 501-682-1529
Website: www.asl.lib.ar.us/

California
California State Archives
1020 "O" St.
Sacramento, CA 95814
Phone: 916-653-7715
Fax: 916-653-7363
E-mail: archivesweb@ss.ca.gov
Website: www.library.ca.gov/

Colorado
Colorado State Library
201 E. Colfax Ave., Rm. 309
Denver, CO 80203
Phone: 303-866-6900
Fax: 303-866-6940
Website: www.cde.state.co.us/index_library.htm

Connecticut
Connecticut State Library
231 Capitol Ave.
Hartford, CT 06106
Phone: 860-757-6500
Website: www.cslib.org/

Delaware
State Library of Delaware
43 S. DuPont Hwy.
Dover, DE 19901
Phone: 302-739-4748
Fax: 302-739-6787
Website: www.lib.de.us/

Florida
State Library of Florida
500 S. Bronough St.
R.A. Gray Gldg.
Tallahassee, FL 32399-0250
Phone: 850-245-6600
Website: dlis.dos.state.fl.us/stlib/

Georgia
State Library of Georgia
1800Century Pl., Ste. 150
Atlanta, GA 30345-4304
Phone: 404-982-3560
Fax: 404-982-3563
Website: www.public.lib.ga.us/

Hawaii
Hawaii State Public Library System
Website: www.hcc.hawaii.edu/hspls/

Idaho
Idaho State Library
325 W. State St.
Boise, IA 83702
Phone: 208-334-2150
Fax: 208-334-4016
Website: www.lili.org/isl/hp.htm

Illinois
Illinois State Library
300 S. 2nd St.
Springfield, IL 62701-1796
Phone: 217-785-5600
Website: www.sos.state.il.us/depts/library/isl_home.html

Indiana
Indiana State Library
140 N. Senate Ave.
Indianapolis, IN 46204-2207
Phone: 317-232-3675
Website: www.statelib.lib.in.us/

Iowa
State Library of Iowa
1112 E. Grand Ave.
Des Moines, IA 50319
Phone: 515-281-4105
Website: www.silo.lib.ia.us/

Kansas
Kansas State Library
300 S.W. Tenth Ave., Rm. 343-N
Topeka, KS 66612-1593
Phone: 785-296-3296
        800-432-3919
Fax: 785-296-6650
Website: skyways.lib.ks.us/kansas/KSL/

Kentucky
Kentucky Department for Libraries and Archives
300 Coffee Tree Rd.
Frankfort, KY 40601
Phone: 502-564-8300
Website: www.kdla.state.ky.us/

Louisiana

State Library of Louisiana
701 N. 4th St.
Baton Rouge, LA 70802
Phone: 225-342-4923
Fax: 225-219-4804
Website: smt.state.lib.la.us/

Maine

Maine State Library
LMA Cultural Building
State House Station #64
Augusta, ME 04333
Phone: 207-287-5600
Fax: 207-287-5615
Website: www.state.me.us/msl/mslhome.htm

Maryland

State Library Resource Center – Central Library
Enoch Pratt Free Library
400 Cathedral St.
Baltimore, MD 21201
Phone: 410-396-5430
E-mail: geninfo@mail.pratt.lib.md.us
Website: www.sailor.lib.md.us/

Massachusetts

State Library of Massachusetts
The George Fingold Library

State House Rm. 341
Boston, MA 02133
Phone: 617-727-2590
Fax: 617-727-5819
Website: www.state.ma.us/lib/

Michigan
Library of Michigan
717 W. Allegan St.
P.O. Box 30007
Lansing, MI 48909-7507
Phone: 517-373-1580
Fax: 517-373-5700
Website: www.libofmich.lib.mi.us/

Minnesota
Minnesota Historical Society
345 Kellogg Blvd. West
St. Paul, MN 55102-1906
Phone: 651-296-2143
Fax: 651-297-7436
Website: www.state.mn.us/libraries/calco.html

Mississippi
Mississippi Library Commission
Website: www.mlc.lib.ms.us/

Missouri
Missouri State Library
P.O. Box 387
Jefferson City, MO 65102-0387
Phone: 573-751-6018
Fax: 573-751-3612
Website: mosl.sos.state.mo.us/lib-ser/libser.html

Montana
Montana State Library
1515 6th Ave.
P.O. Box 201800
Helena, MT 59620-1800
Phone: 406-444-3115
Fax: 406-444-5612
Website: msl.state.mt.us/

Nebraska
Nebraska State Library
State Capitol Bldg., Rm. 325
15th & K Sts.
Lincoln, NE 68509-8931
Phone: 402-471-3189
Fax: 402-471-1011
Website: www.nlc.state.ne.us/

Nevada
Nevada State Library and Archives
100 N. Stewart St.

Carson City, NV 89701-4285
Phone: 775-684-3360
Fax: 775-684-3330
Website: dmla.clan.lib.nv.us/docs/nsla/default.htm

New Hampshire
New Hampshire State Library
20 Park St.
Concord, NH 033301
Phone: 603-271-2392
Fax: 603-271-6826
Website: www.state.nh.us/nhsl/index.html

New Jersey
New Jersey State Library
185 W. State St.
Trenton, NJ 08625-0520
Phone: 609-292-6220
Website: state.nj.us/statelibrary/njlib.htm

New Mexico
New Mexico State Library
1209 Camino Carlos Rey
Santa Fe, NM 87507
Phone: 505-476-9700
Fax: 505-476-9701
Website: www.stlib.state.nm.us/

New York
New York State Library
Cultural Education Center
Empire State Plaza
Albany, NY 12230
Phone: 518-474-5355
Website: www.nysl.nysed.gov/

North Carolina
State Library of North Carolina
109 E. Jones St.
Raleigh, NC 27699
Phone: 919-733-3270
Fax: 919-733-5679
Website: statelibrary.dcr.state.nc.us/

North Dakota
North Dakota State Library
604 E. Boulevard Ave., Dept. 250
Bismarck, ND 58505-0800
Phone: 701-328-4622
Website: ndls.lib.state.nd.us/

Ohio
State Library of Ohio
274 E. First Ave.
Columbus, OH 43201
Phone: 614-644-7061
Fax: 614-466-3584
Website: winslo.state.oh.us

Oklahoma
Oklahoma Department of Libraries
200 NE 18th St.
Oklahoma City, OK 73105-3298
Phone: 405-521-2502
Fax: 405-525-7804
Website: www.odl.state.ok.us/

Oregon
Oregon State Library
250 Winter St. NE
Salem, OR 97301-3950
Phone: 503-378-4243
Website: www.osl.state.or.us/oslhome.html

Pennsylvania
State Library of Pennsylvania
Commonwealth & Walnut Sts.
Harrisburg, PA 17105
Phone: 717-783-5950
E-mail: ra-reference@state.pa.us
Website: www.statelibrary.state.pa.us/libstate.htm

Rhode Island
Rhode Island State Library
State House
Providence, RI 02908
Phone: 401-222-2473
Fax: 401-222-3034

E-mail: tevans@sec.state.ri.us
Website: www.sec.state.ri.us/library/web.htm

South Carolina
South Caroline State Library
Senate & Bull Sts.
Columbia, SC
Phone: 803-734-8666
Fax: 803-734-8676
Website: www.state.sc.us/scsl/

South Dakota
South Dakota State Library
Mercedes MacKay Bldg.
800 Governors Dr.
Pierre, SD 57501-2294
Phone: 605-773-3131
Fax: 605-773-4950
E-Mail: library@state.sd.us
Website: www.state.sd.us/state/executive/deca/
st_lib/st_lib.htm

Tennessee
Tennessee State Library and Archives
403 Seventh Ave. North
Nashville, TN 37243-2764
Phone: 615-741-2764
Website: www.state.tn.us/sos/statelib/tslahome.htm

Texas
Texas State Electronic Library
Website: www.tsl.state.tx.us/

Utah
Utah State Library Division
250 N. 1950 W, Suite A
Salt Lake City, UT 84116-7901
Phone: 801-715-6777
Website: www.state.lib.ut.us/

Vermont
Vermont State Archives
Montpelier, VT 05602
Phone: 802-828-2308
Website: dol.state.vt.us/

Virginia
The Library of Virginia
800 E. Broad St.
Richmond, VA 23219-8000
Phone: 804-692-3500
Website: www.lva.lib.va.us/

Washington
Washington State Library
Point Plaza East
6880 Capitol Blvd. S.
Tumwater, WA 98501-5513

Phone: 360-704-5200
Website: www.state.ib.wa.gov/

Wisconsin
Wisconsin Division for Libraries
Website: www.dpi.state.wi.us/dpi/dltcl/index.html

Wyoming
Wyoming State Library
2301 Capitol Ave.
Cheyenne, WY 82002-0060
Phone: 307-777-7283
Fax: 307-777-6289
Website: www-wsl/state/wy/us/

Vital Records Offices

Birth certificates may tell you if the children who lived in your house were actually born in the house. Death certificates often give the occupation of the deceased. Some Vital Records Departments may have alphabetical indexes; others may not be able to find records unless you supply the name and the date of the birth or death.

Alabama
Center for Health Statistics
State Department of Public Health
P. O. Box 5625

434 Monroe Street
Montgomery, AL 36130
334-206-5418
Marriage: 1936–
Birth and death: 1908–
Divorce: 1950–

Alaska
Department of Health
Sciences and Social Services
Bureau of Vital Statistics
P. O. Box 110675
Juneau, AK 99811
907-465-3391
Marriage, birth, and death: 1913–

Arizona
Vital Records Section
Arizona Department of Health Services
P. O. Box 3887
Phoenix, AZ 85030
602-255-3260
Marriage and divorce: Write county
Birth and death: 1909–

Arkansas
Division of Vital Records
Arkansas Department of Health
4815 West Markham Street

Little Rock, AR 72201
501-661-2336
Marriage: 1917–
Birth and death: 1914–
Divorce: 1923–

California
Vital Statistics Section
Department of Health Services
410 N. Street
P. O. Box 730241
Sacramento, CA 94244
916-445-2684
Marriage, birth, and death: 1905–

Colorado
Vital Records Section
Colorado Department of Health
4300 Cherry Creek Drive South
Denver, CO 80246
303-756-4454
www.cdphe.state.co.us/hs/cshom.html
Marriage and death: 1900–
Birth: 1910

Connecticut
Vital Records
Department of Health Services
410 Capitol Ave.

Hartford, CT 06134
203-566-1124
Send request to town where event occurred.

Delaware
Office of Vital Statistics
Division of Public Health
P. O. Box 637
Dover, DE 19903
302-739-4721
Marriage: 1958–
Birth: 1926–
Death: 1958–

For earlier years, contact:
Archives Hall of Records
Dover, DE
302-739-5318

District of Columbia
Vital Records Branch
800 9th Street, SW.
Washington, DC 20024
202-645-5962
Birth: 1874–
Death: 1855–

For marriages, contact:
Marriage Bureau
515 5th Street, NW
Washington, DC 20001

Florida
Department of Health
Office of Vital Statistics
1217 Pearl Street
P. O. Box 210
Jacksonville, FL 32231
904-359-6900
Marriage: 1927–
Birth: 1865–
Death: 1877–
The majority of birth and death records date from 1917.

Georgia
Department of Human Resources
Vital Records Unit
Room 217-H
47 Trinity Avenue SW
Atlanta, GA 30334
404-656-4900
Marriage and divorce: 1952– (Requests for earlier dates will be forwarded to appropriate county)
Birth and death: 1919–

Hawaii

Office of Health Status
State Department of Health
P. O. Box 3378
Honolulu, HI 96801
808-586-4533
www.hawaii.gov/health/sdohpg02.htm
Marriage, birth, and death: 1853–
Divorce: 1951–

Idaho

Vital Statistics Unit
Department of Health and Welfare
450 West State Street
Boise, ID 83720
208-334-5988
Marriage and divorce: 1947–
Birth and death: 1911–

Illinois

Division of Vital Records
Department of Public Health
605 West Jefferson Street
Springfield, IL 62702
217-782-6553
Marriage and divorce: 1962–
Birth and death: 1916–

Indiana
Vital Records Section
State Department of Health
2 North Median Street
Indianapolis, IN 46204
317-233-2700
www.state.in.us/doh/index.html
Marriage: 1958–
Birth and death: 1907–

Iowa
Department of Public Health
Vital Records Section
Lucas Office Building
321 East 12th Street
Des Moines, IA 50319
515-281-4944
www.idph.state.ia.us/pa/vr.htm
Marriage, birth, and death: 1880–

Kansas
Office of Vital Statistics
State Department of Health and Environment
900 Jackson Street, SW
Topeka, KS 66612
785-296-1400
Marriage: 1913–
Birth and death: 1911–

Kentucky
Office of Vital Statistics
Department for Health Services
275 East Main Street
Frankfort, KY 40621
502-564-4212
Marriage: 1958–
Birth and death: 1911–

Louisiana
Vital Records Registry
Office of Public Health
325 Loyola Avenue
New Orleans, LA 70112
504-568-5152
Marriage: Contact parish
Birth and death: 1914–

City of New Orleans only
Bureau of Vital Statistics
City of Health Department
City Hall
Civic Center
New Orleans, LA 70112
Birth: 1892–
Death: 1942–

Older records for Louisiana can be found at:
Louisiana State Archives

P. O. Box 94125
Baton Rouge, LA 70804

Maine
Office of Vital Records
Human Services Building
Station 11
State House
Augusta, ME 04333
207-287-3181
Marriage, birth, and death: 1892–

Maryland
Division of Vital Records
Department of Health and Mental Hygiene
P. O. Box 68760
Baltimore, MD 21215
410-764-3038
Marriage: 1951–
Birth and death: 1898–

See also:
State of Maryland Archives
350 Rowe Blvd.
Annapolis, MD 21401
410-974-3914

City of Baltimore only
Bureau of Vital Statistics

Municipal Office Building
Baltimore, MD 21202
Birth and death: 1875–

Massachusetts
Registry of Vital Records and Statistics
470 Atlantic Avenue
Boston, MA 02110
617-753-8600
Marriage, birth, and death: 1906–

For earlier records, contact:
The Massachusetts Archives at Columbia Point
220 Morrissey Boulevard
Boston, MA 02125
617-727-2816

Michigan
Office of the State Registrar
Department of Public Health
3423 North Martin Luther King Boulevard
Lansing, MI 48909
517-335-8656
www.mdch.state.mi.us/pha/osr
Marriage, birth, and death: 1867–

Minnesota
Department of Health
Section of Vital Statistics

717 Delaware Street SE
P. O. Box 9441
Minneapolis, MN 55440
612-676-5120
www.health.state.mn.us
Marriage: 1958–
Birth: 1900–
Death: 1908–

Mississippi
Vital Records
State Department of Health
2423 North State Street
Jackson, MS 39216
601-576-7981
Marriage: 1926–1938; 1942–
Birth and death: 1912–

Missouri
Department of Health
Bureau of Vital Records
P. O. Box 570
Jefferson City, MO 65102
573-751-6400
Marriage: 1948–
Birth and death: 1910–
www.health.state.mo.us/cgi-bin/uncgi/Birth
andDeathRecords

Montana
Vital Statistics Bureau
Public Health and Human Services
1400 Broadway
P. O. Box4210
Helena, MT 59604
406-444-4228
www.dphhs.mt.gov
Marriage: 1943–
Birth and death: 1907–

Nebraska
Bureau of Vital Statistics
State Department of Health
301 Centennial Mall South
P. O. Box 95065
Lincoln, NE 68509
402-471-2871
Marriage: 1909–
Birth and death: 1904–

Nevada
Division of Health – Vital Statistics
Capitol Complex
505 East King Street, #102
Carson City, NV 89710
775-687-4480
Marriage: Contact county
Birth and death: 1911

New Hampshire
Bureau of Vital Records
Health and Human Services Building
6 Hazen Drive
Concord, NH 03301
603-271-4654
Marriage, birth, and death: 1640–

New Jersey
State Department of Health
Bureau of Vital Statistics
P. O. Box 370
Trenton, NJ 08625
609-292-4087
Marriage, birth and death: 1878–

For earlier dates, contact:
New Jersey Department of State Division of
Archives and Records Management
P. O. Box 307
Trenton, NJ 08625-0307

New Mexico
Vital Statistics
Health Services Division
P. O. Box 26110
Santa Fe, NM 87502
505-827-2338
Marriage: Contact county
Birth and death: 1880–

New York
Vital Records Section
P. O. Box 2602
Albany, NY 12220
518-474-3075
Marriage, birth, and death: 1880–

For records before this date, contact the Registrar of Vital Statistics in each city and for records pertaining to New York City, contact:
Office of Vital Records
Department of Health
125 Worth Street, , Box 4
New York, NY 10013
212-788-4520
www.ci.nyc.ny.us/health

North Carolina
Vital Records Section
P. O. Box 29537
Raleigh, NC 27626
919-733-3526
Marriage: 1962–
Birth: 1913–
Death: 1946–

Death records from 1913–1945 are at:
North Carolina State Archives
109 East Jones Street

Raleigh, NC 27601
919-733-3526
schs.state.nc.us/SCHS

North Dakota
Division of Vital Records
State Capitol
600 East Boulevard Avenue
Bismarck, ND 58505
701-328-2360
Marriage: 1925–
Birth and death: 1893–

Ohio
Vital Statistics
Department of Health
P. O. Box 15098
Columbus, OH 43215
614-466-2531
Marriage: 1849–
Birth: 1908–
Death: 1936

Earlier records are at:
Ohio Historical Society
Archives Library
1985 Velma Avenue
Columbus, OH 43211

Oklahoma
Vital Records Section
State Department of Health
1000 Northeast 10th Street
P. O. Box 53551
Oklahoma City, OK 73152
405-271-4040
Marriage: at county
Birth and death: 1908–

Oregon
Oregon Health Division
Vital Statistics Section
P. O. Box 14050
Portland, OR 97293
503-731-4095
www.ohd.hr.state.or.us
Marriage: 1906–
Birth and death: 1903–

Pennsylvania
Division of Vital Records
State Department of Health
Central Building
101 South Mercer Street
P. O. Box 1528
New Castle, PA 16103
724-656-3100
Marriage: 1941–
Birth and death: 1906–

Rhode Island
Division of Vital Records
Department of Health
Cannon Building, #101
3 Capital Hill
Providence, RI 02908
401-277-2811
Marriage, birth, and death: 1853–

For records 100 years or less, write above; for earlier ones contact:
State Archives
337 Westminister Street
Providence, RI 02903.

South Carolina
Office of Vital Records
Department of Health and Environmental Control
2600 Bull Street
Columbia, SC 29201
803-734-4830
Marriage: 1950–
Birth and death: 1915–

South Dakota
Department of Health
Vital Records
523 East Capitol
Pierre, SC 57501

605-733-3355
www.state.sd.us/doh/vitalrec/vital.htm
Marriage, birth, and death: 1905–

Tennessee
Vital Records
Department of Health and Environment
421 5th Avenue, North
Nashville, TN 37247
615-741-1763
www.state.tn.us/health/vr/index.html
Marriage: Last 50 years
Birth and death: 1914–

For earlier records, contact:
Tennessee Library
Archives Division
Nashville, TN 37243

Texas
Bureau of Vital Statistics
Department of Health
P. O. Box 12040
Austin, TX 78711
512-458-7111
www.tdh.state.tx.us/bvs
Marriage: 1966–
Birth and death: 1903–

Utah

Bureau of Vital Records
Utah Department of Health
288 North 1460 West
P. O. Box 141012
Salt Lake City, UT 84114
801-538-6105
hlunix.ex.state.ut.us/bvr/home.html
Marriage: 1978–
Birth and death: 1905–

Vermont

Department of Health
Vital Records Section
P. O. Box 70
Burlington, VT 05402
802-863-7275
Keeps only last 10 years of records

For earlier records:
Division of Public Records
US Route 2-Middlesex
Drawer 33
Montpelier, VT 05633
Marriage: 1857–
Birth and death: 1760–

Virginia

Division of Vital Records

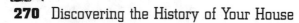

State Health Department
P. O. Box 1000
Richmond, VA 23218
804-225-5000
Marriage, birth, and death: 1853

Washington
Vital Records
1112 South Quince
P. O. Box 9709
Olympia, WA 98507
360-236-4300
www.doh.wa.gov/Topics/chs-cert.html
Marriage: 1968–
Birth and death: 1907–

West Virginia
Vital Registration Office
Division of Health
State Capital Complex
Building 3
Charleston, WV 25305
304-558-2931
Marriage: 1921
Birth and death: 1917

Wisconsin
Vital Records
1 West Wilson Street

P. O. Box 309

Madison, WI 53701

608-266-1371

www.dhfs.state.wi.us/vitalrecords/index.htm

Marriage: Many dating to 1836, complete starting 1907—

Birth and death: Many dating to 1856, complete starting 1907—

Wyoming

Vital Records Services

Hathaway Building

Cheyenne, WY 82002

307-777-7591

Marriage: 1941—

Birth and death: 1909—

Glossary

Abstract of Title – A short history of the owners of a piece of property. Check the documents that you received when you bought your house. A title abstract can be very useful in your research.

Acre – A piece of land containing 10 square chains or 160 square rods (43,560 square feet); approx. 208 feet square.

Agreement (Agt, Agmt) – A legal document made between a grantor (seller) and a grantee (buyer); it may or may not involve a transfer of title. Agreements are worth looking at as they may contain information about the home's architect, the price of home, etc.

Assign – Property owners can assign (transfer) their ownership of land to another person or a company.

Assignment – A document that shows a property owner transferring his or her ownership to another person or a company.

Block – When a piece of land is subdivided, it is generally divided into blocks. Each block is then divided into lots. A parcel or piece of property may include one lot or more, or part of a lot, or parts of two or more lots.

Chain – 4 rods, 100 links, or 66 feet.

Chattel Mortgage – This involves something other than real estate. It does not apply to land.

Circuit Court – A court that has jurisdiction over one or more counties or districts.

Consideration – This usually refers to money that is given as payment for a piece of property, but can mean anything of value that is exchanged for a piece of property.

Convey – To convey property means to transfer ownership of the property from one person to another.

Dedication – A piece of land that is used as a public road, alley, etc. Also called a public easement.

Deed (D) – A legal document that conveys property from grantor (seller) to grantee (buyer), but does not contain a warranty (guarantee) that the grantor owns the property.

Deed in Trust (D in T) – A legal document in which the grantor (property owner) conveys title to the property to a trustee (grantee) to manage for the grantor; trustees usually have the power to rent, sell, or subdivide the property. The trustee is basically the property manager, not the property owner.

Domicile – A permanent dwelling place. Also called a residence.

Easement – Property owners sometimes give easements to electric or telephone companies. These easements allow the companies to use part of the property for overhead lines or underground cables.

Foreclosure – When a property owner does not repay a mortgage on schedule, the lender may force the owner to sell the property to repay the debt.

Grantee – On a deed, the grantee is the buyer. On a mortgage or trust deed, however, the grantee is the person or institution who is lending money to the property owner. The grantee receives the owner's promise to repay the money.

Grantor – On a deed, the grantor is the seller. On a mortgage or trust deed, the grantor is the property owner. The property owner is granting (giving) a promise to repay the money she/he is borrowing.

Hereditaments – Anything that can be inherited – including property.

Improvements – Anything that is added to or upgrades a piece of property. Improvements could include the clearing and cultivating of land, planting trees, building roads or houses, installing sewer or water lines, etc.

Instrument – A legal document.

Intestate – When a person dies without leaving a valid will, that person is said to have died "intestate."

Joint Tenancy – This occurs when two people own one piece of property. When one person dies, the other automatically inherits the property.

Lien – A lien on a piece of property means that the owner owes money to someone else. When the property is sold, that other person will receive the money that he or she is owed.

Link – 1/25 of a rod, 1/100 of a chain, or 7.92 inches.

Lis Pendens – This means that there is a lawsuit in progress that involves this piece of property.

Lot – A piece of land on a block. Subdividers divide land into blocks, and each block is divided into lots.

Mile – 80 chains, or 320 rods, or 5,280 feet.

Mechanic's Lien (ML) – If a tradesperson works on a home and is not paid in full, he/she can file a mechanic's lien (a legal document) so that when the property owner sells the property, the tradesperson will be paid off at the closing.

Mortgage (Mtg.) – A legal document in which the grantor (property) owner gives the mortgage (a promise to repay money) to the grantee (lending institution). Technically, you do not get a mortgage from a bank, you give a mortgage to a bank.

Parcel – Property; a piece of land. A parcel may be one lot or several lots on subdivided land, or it may be a piece of land that is not subdivided.

Premises – Land and anything that is built on it such as a house, barn, garage, windmill, etc. When deeds refer to premises, it does not necessarily mean that a house exists.

Property – Anything that can be owned, including land and houses.

Public Easement – A piece of land that is used as a public road, alley, etc. Also called a dedication.

Quit Claim Deed (QCD) – A legal document in which the grantor gives up all claims to a piece of property to the grantee. Sometimes the grantor does not own the property; he/she often owns a lot of property in the area.

Release (Rel.) – A legal document in which the grantor (lender or lending institution) gives a release to a grantee (property owner who had borrowed money from the grantor) stating that the money has been paid in full. When a mortgage is paid off, the lending institution gives the property owner a release.

Residence – A permanent dwelling place. Also called a domicile.

Riparian Rights – People who own land on the banks of a lake or river generally have the right to use this waterway.

Rod – 25 links, or 1/4 of a chain, or 16.5 feet.

Section – A one-mile square piece of land; contains 640 acres.

Sheriff's Deed (SD) – A legal document often used to convey property that is auctioned off to the highest bidder, sometimes for non-payment of taxes. The delinquent taxpayer can buy back the property if he/she pays the taxes plus a fine within a year or two.

Title Search – A search made in a recorder of deeds office to determine who is the legal property owner, and to see if anyone else has any claims on the property via a lien, mortgage, etc.

Township – A piece of land that is six miles square, and formed by township and range lines. A township contains 36 square miles (36 sections); do not confuse this with named townships of today.

Trust Deed (TD) – A legal document that is similar to a mortgage; it is still used today, but was more common before 1900. The grantor (property owner) gives the trust deed (a promise to pay back money) to the grantee (the money lender).

Warranty Deed (WD) – A legal document in which a grantor (seller) transfers property (with a guarantee that he/she really owns that property) to the grantee (buyer).

Bibliography

Alabama Historical Commission, National Register Division. *A Guide to Researching Old Buildings in Alabama*. Alabama: Alabama Historical Commission, n.d.

Attebery, Jennifer Eastman and Ford, Guila. *A Guide to Documenting the History of a Building*. Reference Series 741. Idaho: Idaho State Historical Society, 1983.

Burkhardt, Ann McCorquodale. *House Detective: Guide to Researching Birmingham Buildings*. Alabama: Birmingham Historical Society, 1988.

Cesna, Valerie and Brizolara, Susan. *How to Research the History of Your Home in New Castle County, Delaware*. Delaware: New Castle County Department of Planning, 1996.

Charlotte-Mecklenburn Historic Landmarks Commission. *How to Research the History of Real Estate,* n.d. www.cmhpf.org/resources/researching.html

Colorado Historical Society. *Researching the History of Your House.* Colorado: Colorado Historical Society, 1999.

Compau, Nancy. Historic *House Research Guide.* Washington: City of Spokane, 1999. www.historic spokane.org/guide34.htm

Cunnington, Pamela. *How Old is Your House?* Sherborne, Eng.: Alphabooks, 1980.

Everard, Wayne M. *How to Research the History of Your House (or Other Building) in New Orleans.* New Orleans: Friends of New Orleans Public Library, 1986.

Greene County Public Library (Ohio). *Dating a Structure,* n.d. www.gcpl.lib.oh.us/services/ger/hist_res/ dating.html

Historic Landmarks Foundation of Indiana, Indiana Historical Bureau. *Historic House Research Handbook: Focus on Local History, Number 1.* Indiana: Historic Landmarks Foundation of Indiana, 1993.

Houck, Maurcia DeLean. *If These Walls Could Talk...* Rockport, ME: Picton Press, 1999.

Houses in a Box. Atglen, PA: Schiffer Publishing Ltd., 1998.

Howard, Hugh. *How Old is This House?* New York: Noonday Press, 1989.

Howe, Barbara J. *Houses and Homes: Exploring Their History.* Walnut Creek, CA: Alta Mira Press, 1997.

Indianapolis Historic Preservation Commission. *Handbook for Historical Building Research.* Indiana: Indianapolis Historic Preservation Commission, n.d.

Iredale, David. *Discovering Your Old House.* Aylesbury: Shire Publications, 1991.

Kansas State Historical Society. *Guide to Research Resources in the Library and Archives Division of the Kansas State Historical Society.* Kansas: Kansas State Historical Society, 1997.

Kansas State Historical Society. *Researching Old Buildings.* Kansas: Kansas State Historical Society, n.d.

Koos, Greg. *Researching Your Illinois House.* Springfield, Illinois: Illinois Historic Preservation Agency, 1986.

Lamar, Christine, ed. *Uncovering the History of Your House.* Providence, Rhode Island: Rhode Island Historical Society, 1987.

Light, Sally. *House Histories: A Guide to Tracing the Genealogy of Your Home.* Spencertown, NY: Golden Hill Press, 1989.

McAlester, Virginia & Lee. *A Field Guide to American Houses.* New York: Alfred A. Knopf, 1991.

McHugh, Floyd. *Sources & Searches: Documenting Historic Buildings in New Mexico.* New Mexico: New Mexico Historic Preservation Division, 1985.

McIntyre Library, University of Wisconsin, Eau Claire. *Tracing the History of Your House,* n.d. www. uwec.edu/library/guides/househist.html

Montana Historical Society. *National Register of Historic Places Workbook.* Montana: Montana Historical Society, State Historic Preservation Office, n.d.

Munger, Donna Bingham. *Pennsylvania Land Records: A History and Guide for Research.* Pennsylvania: Pennsylvania Historical and Museum Commission, 1991.

Nevada State Historic Preservation Office. *How to Prepare Nominations to the National Register of Historic Places: A Guide for Nevada Property Owners.* Nevada: Nevada State Historic Preservation Office, 1999.

O'Donnell, Eleanor. *Researching a Historic Property: National Register Bulletin.* No. 39, n.d.

Powell, John Edward and Enns-Rempel, Kevin. *Historic Residence Research Resources: A Guide for the Layperson to Sources of Building Data in Fresno*, n.d. www.fresno.edu/preserve/resource.htm.

Schweitzer, Robert et al. *America's Favorite Homes.* Detroit, MI: Wayne State University Press, 1990.

Sears, Roebuck Catalog of Houses 1926. NY: Dover Publications, 1991.

State Historical Society of Wisconsin. *Researching Old Buildings.* Wisconsin: State Historical Society of Wisconsin, 1996.

Stevenson, Katherine Cole et al. *Houses By Mail.* Washington, D.C.: Preservation Press, 1986.

Texas Historical Commission. *Texas Preservation Guidelines – Remembering Texas: Guidelines for Historic Research.* Texas: Texas Historical Commission, 1998.

Thomas, Jr., Ken H. *Documenting a Historic Structure in Atlanta.* Historic Preservation Division, Georgia Department of Natural Resources, n.d.

Utah Office of Preservation. *Intensive Level Survey: Standard Operating Procedures.* Utah: Utah Office of Preservation, 1993.

Webber, Joan. *How Old is Your House?* Chester, Conn: Pequot Press, 1978.

Index

BOOK DESCRIPTIONS

Blues for Bird
by Martin Gray
288 pages $16.95

The Book of Good Habits
*Simple and Creative Ways
to Enrich Your Life*
by Dirk Mathison
224 pages $9.95

The Butt Hello
*and other ways my cats
drive me crazy*
by Ted Meyer
96 pages $9.95

Café Nation
*Coffee Folklore, Magick,
and Divination*
by Sandra Mizumoto Posey
224 pages $9.95

**Discovering the History
of Your House**
and Your Neighborhood
by Betsy J. Green
288 pages $14.95

Exploring Our Lives
*A Writing Handbook for
Senior Americans*
by Francis E. Kazemek
288 pages $14.95

Footsteps in the Fog
*Alfred Hitchcock's
San Francisco*
by Jeff Kraft and
Aaron Leventhal
240 pages $24.95

**FREE Stuff & Good Deals
for Folks over 50**
by Linda Bowman
240 pages $12.95

**FREE Stuff & Good Deals
for Your Kids**
by Linda Bowman
240 pages $12.95

**FREE Stuff & Good Deals
for Your Pet**
by Linda Bowman
240 pages $12.95

**FREE Stuff & Good Deals
on the Internet**
by Linda Bowman
240 pages $12.95

Helpful Household Hints
*The Ultimate Guide
to Housekeeping*
by June King
224 pages $12.95

**How to Find Your Family
Roots and Write Your
Family History**
by William Latham and
Cindy Higgins
288 pages $14.95

How to Speak Shakespeare
by Cal Pritner and
Louis Colaianni
144 pages $16.95

**How to Win Lotteries,
Sweepstakes, and Contests
in the 21st Century**
by Steve "America's
Sweepstakes King" Ledoux
224 pages $14.95

The Keystone Kid
Tales of Early Hollywood
by Coy Watson, Jr.
312 pages $24.95

Letter Writing Made Easy!
*Featuring Sample Letters for
Hundreds of Common Occasions*
by Margaret McCarthy
224 pages $12.95

**Letter Writing Made Easy!
Volume 2**
*Featuring More Sample Letters for
Hundreds of Common Occasions*
by Margaret McCarthy
224 pages $12.95

**Nancy Shavick's Tarot
Universe**
by Nancy Shavick
336 pages $15.95

Offbeat Food
*Adventures in an
Omnivorous World*
by Alan Ridenour
240 pages $19.95

Offbeat Golf
*A Swingin' Guide to a
Worldwide Obsession*
by Bob Loeffelbein
192 pages $17.95

Offbeat Marijuana
*The Life and Times of the
World's Grooviest Plant*
by Saul Rubin
240 pages $19.95

Offbeat Museums
*The Collections and Curators of
America's Most Unusual Museums*
by Saul Rubin
240 pages $19.95

Past Imperfect
*How Tracing Your Family Medical
History Can Save Your Life*
by Carol Daus
240 pages $12.95

Quack!
*Tales of Medical Fraud from
the Museum of Questionable
Medical Devices*
by Bob McCoy
240 pages $19.95

**The Seven Sacred Rites
of Menarche**
*The Spiritual Journey of the
Adolescent Girl*
by Kristi Meisenbach Boylan
160 pages $11.95

**The Seven Sacred Rites
of Menopause**
*The Spiritual Journey to
the Wise-Woman Years*
by Kristi Meisenbach Boylan
144 pages $11.95

Silent Echoes
*Discovering Early Hollywood
Through the Films of Buster Keaton*
by John Bengtson
240 pages $24.95

What's Buggin' You?
*Michael Bohdan's Guide to
Home Pest Control*
by Michael Bohdan
256 pages $12.95

ORDER FORM 1-800-784-9553

	Quantity	Amount
Blues for Bird ($16.95)		
The Book of Good Habits ($9.95)		
The Butt Hello ($9.95)		
Café Nation ($9.95)		
Discovering the History of Your House . . . ($14.95)		
Exploring Our Lives ($14.95)		
Footsteps in the Fog ($24.95)		
FREE Stuff & Good Deals for Folks over 50 ($12.95)		
FREE Stuff & Good Deals for Your Kids ($12.95)		
FREE Stuff & Good Deals for Your Pet ($12.95)		
FREE Stuff & Good Deals on the Internet ($12.95)		
Helpful Household Hints ($12.95)		
How to Find Your Family Roots . . . ($14.95)		
How to Speak Shakespeare ($16.95)		
How to Win Lotteries, Sweepstakes, and Contests. . . ($14.95)		
The Keystone Kid ($24.95)		
Letter Writing Made Easy! ($12.95)		
Letter Writing Made Easy! Volume 2 ($12.95)		
Nancy Shavick's Tarot Universe ($15.95)		
Offbeat Food ($19.95)		
Offbeat Golf ($17.95)		
Offbeat Marijuana ($19.95)		
Offbeat Museums ($19.95)		
Past Imperfect ($12.95)		
Quack! ($19.95)		
The Seven Sacred Rites of Menarche ($11.95)		
The Seven Sacred Rites of Menopause ($11.95)		
Silent Echoes ($24.95)		
What's Buggin' You? ($12.95)		

	Subtotal	
Shipping & Handling:	**CA residents add 8.25% sales tax**	
1 book **$3.00**	**Shipping and Handling (see left)**	
Each additional book is **$ .50**	**TOTAL**	

Name _____

Address _____

City _____ State _____ Zip _____

☐ Visa ☐ MasterCard   Card No.: _____

Exp. Date _____   Signature _____

☐ Enclosed is my check or money order payable to:

Santa Monica Press LLC
P.O. Box 1076
Santa Monica, CA 90406
www.santamonicapress.com 1-800-784-9553